LANGUAGE AND L

Dorothy S. Stricklar
Celia Genishi and Donna E.

ADVISORY BOARD: Richard Allington, Kathryn Au, Ber
Carole Edelsky, Shirley Brice Heath, Conn

MW00983216

(continued)

For volumes in the NCRLL Collection (edited by JoBeth Allen and Donna E. Alvermann) and the Practitioners Bookshelf Series (edited Celia Genishi and Donna E. Alvermann), as well as a complete list of titles in this series, please visit www.tcpress.com.

Literacy Playshop

New Literacies, Popular Media,
and Play in the
Early Childhood Classroom

Karen E. Wohlwend

Teachers College
Columbia University
New York and London

Published by Teachers College Press, 1234 Amsterdam Avenue, New York, NY 10027

Portions of this research appeared in Husbye, N. E., Buchholz, B. A., Coggin, L. S., Wessel-Powell, C., & Wohlwend, K. E. (2012). Critical lessons and playful literacies: Digital media in the PK–2 classroom. *Language Arts, 90*(2), 82–92. Copyright © 2012 by the National Council of Teachers of English. Reprinted with permission.

Library of Congress Cataloging-in-Publication Data

Wohlwend, Karen E.
   Literacy playshop : new literacies, popular media, and play in the early childhood classroom / Karen E. Wohlwend.
      pages cm. — (Language and literacy series)
   Includes bibliographical references and index.
   ISBN 978-0-8077-5428-3 (pbk. : alk. paper)
   ISBN 978-0-8077-5429-0 (hardcover : alk. paper)
   1. Language arts (Early childhood) 2. Media programs (Education) 3. Play. I. Title.
   LB1139.5.L35W62 2013
   372.6—dc23   2012050134

ISBN 978-0-8077-5428-3 (paperback)
ISBN 978-0-8077-5429-0 (hardcover)

Printed on acid-free paper
Manufactured in the United States of America

20 19 18 17 16 15 14 13   8 7 6 5 4 3 2 1

Contents

Preface

Time for Literacy Play

Time for play is shrinking in early childhood classrooms, even though it's a primary way for children to engage and understand the world around them. In this standards-driven era, it's not enough to argue that play builds social skills or provides physical exercise. Time for play depends on demonstrating its curricular value as a core literacy with growing importance in this century. For example, playing and producing video text are highly effective literacies for communicating on YouTube and Twitter. Children's play and media experiences are a natural starting point for developing their digital literacies.

Children's play worlds are storied worlds with texts filled with vibrant dialogue, characters, and storylines. During play, children make their own imaginary versions of real-life or fantasy worlds but on their own terms, which allows them to make friendships and remake stories to fit their needs. Children's play reflects their immersion in a stream of commercial messages and advertising, including narratives from popular television shows, movies, video games, and toy franchises. Critical approaches seem to have limited impact when pitted against young children's passionate identification with their favorite princesses and superheroes, which are highly valued in their peer cultures (Davies, 2003; Pugh, 2009). But when children play popular media narratives, they can experience firsthand the constraints of stereotypical characters, actions, and plot lines and improvise ways to play around these obstacles. For example, in *Playing Their Way into Literacies* (2011), I described how kindergartners revised passive roles for the Disney princesses they loved when faced with directing peers in a child-produced film while playing an immobilized Sleeping Beauty. Their classroom was a Literacy Playshop, a wonderfully playful space with a creative and responsive teacher where children's developing literacies flourished as they played together and made films with popular media.

I wondered how to help other teachers to create similar Literacy Playshops and to use literacy play to build on the unique strengths of their young students. I began working with teacher study groups to support teachers as they studied popular media and developed literacy play curriculum:

- How can early childhood teachers support children's video explorations, mediate their collaborative film and drama projects, and better understand how children think and make meaning together during play and media production?

- What are the curricular processes in a Literacy Playshop? How do these processes interrelate?
- What kind of collaborative support do teachers and children need?
- How does this kind of media-rich literacy play curriculum function with different age groups in early childhood classrooms?

Because most media production education has targeted older students, one of the challenges in this work is to find tools and, importantly, instructional goals that fit the abilities and strengths of young children (Rogow, 2002). Camera buttons and screens must be large enough for a preschooler's fingers to manipulate and the camera small enough for a preschooler's hand to hold. Similarly, expectations for a child-produced film must match a young child's moment-to-moment goals and fluid storytelling. In the same way, criticality must be reconceptualized for early childhood. Children's responses that seem critical in class discussions may not transfer to their writings or, more important, to their playing of the narratives they know by heart. Early critical literacy begins with an awareness that media's pervasive texts are malleable and can be reinvented by children in collaborative stories, and that such reconstructions happen regularly and naturally in children's play. With these strengths in mind, Literacy Playshop offers curricular activities for early childhood teachers who want to begin a new literacies adventure.

Overview of the Research Project

During the course of 1 school year, six early childhood teachers in three preschool and K-1 classrooms met in study group teams to develop and try out critical and productive approaches to media-rich literacy play curricula. In two preschool classrooms in the same child care center, teachers Dawn Berkenstock, Karen Hahn, Michiru Oleson, and Sara Rush worked with over 40 3- to 5-year-old children who played stories about Dora the Explorer, Transformers, pirates, princesses, and more as they created their own films with popular media toys. At a public charter elementary school across town, teachers Doriet Burkowitz and Elizabeth Winarski developed critical literacy and media production activities for about 50 5- to 7-year-old children in their shared kindergarten-grade 1 classroom.

The families served by the school and child care center in this university town in a U.S. Midwestern state represented a limited range of diversity: children were primarily from White, middle-class families. Many parent were faculty or graduate students; some had transnational or international histories and trajectories. Similarly, the teachers and researchers (discussed in detail in the following paragraph) were primarily White and middle-class; one teacher and two researchers have transnational histories with Japan, China, or Turkey.

Throughout the book, I use the term *we* to recognize the contributions and collaborations among co-researchers Beth Buchholz, Christy Wessel Powell, Nicholas Husbye, and Linda Coggin. Christy, Nicholas, and I facilitated and recorded the study groups, providing professional development and technical support. As the Literacy Playshops unfolded, Christy, Beth, Linda, and five additional graduate students worked in classrooms to record activity, visiting each classroom 2 to 4 days a week during the spring semester.

To explore the possibilities of a playshop approach, we needed to find sites that welcome educational innovation. As a university child care and a public charter school, both settings enjoyed more freedom for creative programming than many under-resourced schools in high-poverty areas that must follow mandated curricula and comply with testing-driven oversight that prohibits or severely limits play activities.

We had three goals for the literacy play curriculum:

1. Draw upon children's expertise and work with peer culture to enrich students' reading and writing and expand their participation in classroom literacy activities (Dyson, 2003a; Fernie, Madrid, & Kantor, 2011).
2. Encourage critical awareness of commercial product messages and help children see popular media (films, video games, toys) as pliable texts that can be revised through playful production to create their own storylines and character identities (Wohlwend, 2011).
3. Incorporate filmmaking as a key literacy activity for producing action texts that integrate play and drama.

Teacher study groups met regularly, about every other week, to read research on critical literacy (Vasquez, 2004), play and popular media (Marsh, 2005a), and media production (Bazalgette, 2010; Riddle, 2009). Teachers also used this time to learn filmmaking techniques, plan classroom activities, talk through issues, and celebrate successes. During the first semester, the teachers acquired skills in filmmaking as they engaged in sample curricular activities such as storyboarding, framing shots, and film editing (for examples, see Component 1 Teacher Inquiry Activities).

In the second semester, the teachers brainstormed and problem-solved class activities. They also shared insights while viewing short video clips of filmmaking activities or student films created in their classrooms. Between study group sessions, we videotaped teachers as they tried out their planned media engagements with their students. For example, in one engagement, children viewed popular films such as Pixar shorts to understand film conventions and composition. Children also collaborated to write scripts, draw storyboards, animate media toys and handmade puppets as main characters, and produce their own films with popular media themes. During classroom visits, we observed and talked with teachers and children, photographed storyboards and writing samples, and videotaped children during dramatic play, storying, and filmmaking activities. Children's activity during play, writing, and filming with media toys was analyzed for mediation levels (teacher-led, tools, and child-led) and processes (playing, storying, collaboration, and media production). Finally, the research team analyzed three sets of video data (child-produced films, classroom filmmaking activity, and teacher study group discussions) to identify and compare patterns across levels and processes.

The Literacy Playshops were emergent, and we all learned along the way. A key strength was the teachers' willingness to explore new literacies and to invent as curricular processes unfolded. Always taking their cues from the children, the teachers listened to their ideas and responded to build on and link children's story-telling strengths and media knowledge to their emergent abilities in media critique and film production and, of course, to school literacy benchmarks and standards.

About This Book

The purpose of this book is to help early childhood teachers develop their own pro-ductive media approach to literacy play curriculum and to show its potential for helping young children respond productively to a world filled with identity texts circulating through media franchises of popular films, television, video games, and more. This book is based on the premise that early childhood educators can proactively support young children's abilities to critically engage media narratives by facilitating children's pretending and remaking of commercial texts. Specifi-cally, educators can help children see themselves as producers and promote critical responses to popular media by demonstrating that widely circulating scripts and character identity messages are subject to change when children play together.

The first part of the book, Chapters 1–4, illustrates the Literacy Playshop framework, in which play and filmmaking act as productive literacies that link to children's popular media passions. These chapters provide rationale for Literacy Playshops and excerpts from the three early childhood classrooms to show how young children developed literacies through media play and emergent filmmak-ing. In Chapter 1, I introduce Literacy Playshop and argue the need for critical and productive media curricula that move beyond a permeable curriculum into "play-ful pedagogies" (Buckingham, 2003, p. 117) that provide very young children with opportunities to mediate—to make meanings accessible, sensible, and usable—as they produce media and transform media texts through play and filmmaking.

Chapter 2 and Chapter 3, written by pairs of co-researchers, describe how teachers who worked with 3- to 7-year-old children in three early childhood class-rooms developed and implemented play-based literacy learning and media pro-duction. Chapter 2 (kindergarten/1st grade) and Chapter 3 (preschool) provide excerpts from early childhood classrooms to show how young children's media play and emergent filmmaking developed and how teachers' notions of media curricula moved from familiar educational models of writing workshops or class pageants to Literacy Playshops. Each playshop was unique, reflecting the character of each educational setting. In Chapter 2, Beth Buchholz and Linda Coggin fore-ground literacy, describing how the K-1 literacy curriculum expanded through play and media production, highlighting how children negotiated gender in their media play and in their relationships with peers. In Chapter 3, Christy Wessel Powell and Nicholas Husbye foreground play, showing how media production was used as a developmentally appropriate literacy to record and enrich preschool children's play and to open opportunities for diverse learners to tap into their technological and popular media expertise.

Chapter 4 provides the theoretical foundation for the Literacy Playshop framework and its three levels (teacher-guided engagements, child explorations, and shared meaning mediators) and four processes (playing, storying, collaboration, and production). The chapter explains the supporting concepts for the model, synthesizing filmmaking processes across levels of mediation and summarizing key insights on creating Literacy Playshops and expanding school literacies.

The second part of the book, divided into Components 1–4, provides activities for each of the three levels and each of the four processes. Component 1 describes teacher inquiry activities to support teacher study groups through professional development activities. Component 2 offers guided engagements with sample curricular activities designed to help children mediate media texts. Component 3 lists the kinds of mediators teachers used to support shared meaning-making, while Component 4 documents the range of children's independent explorations. Technology is a moving target with new apps appearing and others disappearing every day. These dynamic resources are invitations to explore, and so "Technology Try-Its" in each section provide current resources and websites for readers to browse as potential extensions. The sample activities in the four components are provided to inspire and support teachers in designing their own Literacy Playshops.

Acknowledgments

My co-researchers and I are most grateful to the creative and dedicated early childhood teachers who worked in teacher study groups with us for a full academic year to develop and try out ground-breaking curricular ideas and who welcomed our research team into their preschool and kindergarten/1st-grade classrooms to see these exciting literacies in action: Dawn Berkenstock, Doriet Burkowitz, Karen Hahn, Michiru Oleson, Sara Rush, and Elizabeth Winarski.

We are deeply indebted to the contributions of fellow members of the research team who facilitated classroom play and media production, gathered video data carefully, and faithfully cataloged and summarized video each week for an entire semester, but more important, we appreciate their valuable insights and perspectives during our research class discussions. In addition to the chapter co-authors, the research team included Yahya Erbas, Diane Glosson, Kathleen McCormick, Rafi Santo, Samantha Sisk, and Zitong Wei.

This research was supported by a Maris M. Proffitt and Mary Higgins Proffitt Endowment Grant administered through the Indiana University School of Education.

Thanks to acquisition editor Emily Spangler for her ongoing advice and encouragement and to copyeditor Corinne Mooney for her diligent reading and thoughtful suggestions.

Thanks to the National Council of Teachers of English and the editors of *Language Arts* for allowing excerpts from an earlier journal article to be reproduced and expanded in this book.

Literacy Playshop

CHAPTER 1

Playing with and Living in Popular Media

Imagine the variety of popular media products that a preschooler encounters each morning: *Brave* princess pajamas and bedding, *Little Mermaid* toothbrush by the bathroom sink, *Shrek* cereal on the breakfast table, and *Dora the Explorer* in English and Spanish running on television, interrupted by advertisements for fast food, toys, film trailers, and so on. Children don't just view, read, or play commercial messages and scripts from popular media films, television shows, and video games; they live immersed in these texts through omnipresent flows of transmedia—the franchises anchored by children's media (e.g., *Disney Princess, Spider-Man, Toy Story*) that spin off toys, snacks, towels, shoes, shampoo, and other consumer goods. Clearly, children's literacy experiences reach beyond their bedtime stories and even beyond their interactions with television or computer screens.

To be clear, my use of *media* includes image, print, audio, and animated texts such as video that convey meaningful messages, whether produced by children or corporations, while *popular media* indicates a subset of media connected to an anchoring brand, film narrative, television series, or video game. I use *transmedia* to indicate licensed popular media franchises of toys, entertainment products, and consumer goods.

From Markets to Playrooms

Hair-flinging Rapunzel and web-swinging Spider-Man are just two of the thousands of characters in transmedia that cover the taken-for-granted stuff of everyday childhoods. These characters come prepackaged with movie scripts, ad campaigns, and other identity messages that tell young consumers not only what to buy but who they should be and become. The most obvious texts that circulate through transmedia are the film scripts or video game narratives. For example, the storylines in the Disney Princess franchise (e.g., *Tangled, Sleeping Beauty, Snow White and the Seven Dwarfs, The Little Mermaid*) cast girls as damsels in distress and boys as heroic warriors. Disney Pixar's *Brave* (Chapman & Andrews, 2012) is a recent and notable exception with an active princess archer who determines her own destiny sans prince. However, at the time of this writing, Princess Merida has not been officially added to the Disney Princess brand. Transmedia also send messages in other ways, such as film marketing that sends out advance trailers, pop-up ads, and cross-promotions with fast food or other products. These messages focus on target demographics (particular gender, age group, geographic location, income level) and create identity texts that indicate who is expected to be a fan and consumer. For example, it's fairly clear that boys are expected to identify with pirate toys, while girls are expected to identify with princess dolls (Wohlwend & Hubbard, 2011). Identity expectations frame marketing decisions for pink and sparkly packaging on Disney Princess dolls that alerts buyers that this product is intended for girls. In turn, parents and children participate by purchasing and using products in expected ways, thereby validating marketing decisions as consumers buy in and support corporate identity expectations for child consumers. Families further this buy-in by supporting their children's strong attachments to favorite popular media characters so that toys and dolls become necessary artifacts in daily routines and bedtime rituals (Marsh, 2005b).

From Playrooms to Classrooms

Despite the widespread presence of transmedia in children's lives, early childhood classrooms offer few opportunities for children to explore their often passionate attachment to favorite characters and thus to draw upon their literary knowledge of favorite animated films, video games, television shows, or websites (Marsh et al., 2005). Few teachers provide—or even allow children to bring—media toys to classroom play centers, an issue that is further compounded by accountability trends that reduce time for play in early childhood classrooms (Brown, 2009; Schoenberg, 2010). Mandates for basic skills literacy instruction and didactic teaching hit under-resourced schools particularly hard (Dyson, 2008), so that preschoolers who are already disadvantaged by economic hardship get fewer chances to play together in school (Stipek, 2004). Equitable access to play becomes a social justice issue when some children get opportunities to play in school while others do not. Literacy play levels the field by giving children access to their cultural expertise and time to play the stories they know best, whether classic children's books or popular media.

Some teachers steer children away from playing, writing, or drawing about media themes, concerned about parent reactions or enacting their own perceptions that popular media are stereotypical and developmentally inappropriate (too violent, too sexual) for innocent children (Marsh, 2006). These well-intentioned aims to shelter children from inappropriate material are rooted in middle-class beliefs about taste and propriety (Pompe, 1996). The unintended consequence that results: children with fewer economic resources are particularly disadvantaged when transmedia are banned from the classroom:

> The promotional, mass-market toys sold in Toys R Us and most available to and popular with working-class children are the toys most likely to be excluded from the culture of the classroom.... The familiarity of the material objects will be just one of the many advantages that will bear on the child's future success in the classroom. Promotional toys ... are likely to meet a cool reception by teachers.... In an attempt [by the teacher] to censor mass culture, the children most in need of comfort, security and involvement in school are the ones most disadvantaged. (Seiter, 1992, p. 246)

Teachers who participated in our study were chagrined when they realized that the commercial-free stance that prohibited popular media toys in their school distanced children from their home cultures, violating a key mission. Dawn noted, "If I'm not allowing this in, I'm not respecting children's home cultures. [Instead the message is:] What is loving and comfortable doesn't belong here." Through careful kidwatching (Goodman, 1978), she began keeping a record of the transmedia that had permeated her preschool classroom through children's blankets, underwear, and diapers, despite the school's commercial-free stance. Dawn wryly noted that she had a two-page list of popular media products "that don't come into my classroom."

Some teachers feel that they cannot justify taking time for play with transmedia toys ("they get enough of that at home") or that children are just parroting media scripts rather than writing original stories. However, the devaluing of popular media knowledge in classrooms distances children from important literacy resources such as snippets of dialogue, richly developed settings, character personalities, or logical plot organization—all of which are gained through young children's personal experiences viewing favorite films, television programs and commercials, and videogames. Dyson's early childhood classroom studies (2003a, 2006, 2008) demonstrate that children's writing development and social status benefit from a permeable curriculum that allows popular culture to seep into the classroom. My previous research (Wohlwend, 2011) shows that when young children engage in daily, sustained periods of 45 to 60 minutes to play and revisit media themes together, they improvise and create their own characters and revise scripts.

Connecting to other children through shared popular media knowledge is an important way for children to access play groups and reconfigure classroom power relations. For example, the most desired toys become badges of belonging in play groups (Pugh, 2009). When children pick up a popular toy, they also take up its complicated mix of messages. For example, a boy who picks up a Disney Princess doll and wants to play Cinderella must negotiate peers' expectations for girls-only play groups, passive heroine roles, and children's shared play histories (Wohlwend, 2012). Such items of transmedia provide readily available but also problematic identity texts that mingle beloved characters, familiar storylines, gender stereotypes, scripted roles, advertisements, and designs in everyday products that invite players to express fan and consumer identities, affiliate with a particular brand, and enact stereotypical roles.

Introducing Literacy Playshop

To address the realities of childhood today, educators need to think beyond print-intensive literacy skills tasks—or even book-centered reading and writing workshops—and to envision play-enriched new literacies curricula. In other words, we can expand reading and writing workshops into literacy "playshops" (Wohlwend,

2011, p. 121). In this book, my co-researchers and I describe one kind of Literacy Playshop: teacher-designed media-rich playshops where children produce digital film and collaborate as they play together.

The aim of this work is critical, but not through class discussions that deconstruct the gendered or raced stereotypes in popular media and books, an approach that has had limited success with preschoolers (Davies, 2003). Instead, we reconceptualize critical literacy for early childhood education as a play space that opens opportunities for redesign *on children's terms* using the materials and narratives that they know best. We reframe the notion of *critical* for early childhood settings by recognizing that power relations shape children's participation at school. Children's literacy practices and peer histories influence here-and-now conflicts and everyday negotiations as children play, share materials, and work out who should play with which toy (Wohlwend, 2011). When children collaborate during play, storytelling, and media production experiences, they must work out gender issues and media passions enacted through their friendships, character attachments, and co-authoring literacy practices. During Literacy Playshop activities, teachers can reposition children in relation to popular media texts and characters so that children learn to work together productively and think as media producers, not just as consumers. This repositioning opens more equitable ways for diverse learners to perform literate identities by expanding the range of possible entry points and avenues and by recognizing children's popular media passions as valuable *literacy resources*—knowledge about characters, plots, and story structure that can inform children's reading and writing.

Production and Collaboration as Critical Processes. Studies in preschools and kindergartens show that young children can critically engage popular media (Dyson, 2003a) and corporate marketing (Vasquez, 2004) when they play and produce media of their own (Nixon & Comber, 2005; Wohlwend, 2011). Further, when children play gendered, classed, or raced texts in contexts that matter to them, they engage in transformation at the level of lived practices and classroom power relationships (Heffernan & Lewison, 2005; Vasquez, 2004; Wohlwend, 2011). As children collaborate to produce a play scenario or a film, they work through issues of conflict, peer exclusion, and gender expectations while negotiating peer culture relationships (Boldt, 2002). They also must agree upon a shared narrative that brings together their competing ideas for story actions, interpretations of commercial narratives, and notions of what makes sense:

- Who gets to hold the camera?
- Who can play a girl or a boy?
- What character actions are possible and who can authorize changes?
- Who decides?

Such collaborative, productive remakings of popular media requires deep engagement with multiple layers in complex identity texts—the kind of embodied and immersive engagement that play naturally provides.

Play and Filmmaking as Collaborative Literacies. In a climate of high-stakes testing, it may seem risky or frivolous to set aside the scripted teacher's manual, to make room for play with mass-market toys, and to encourage children to explore filmmaking in school. The last section of this book offers strategies that teachers have used to gain parent and administrator support for play-based learning (see Component 1 for the teacher inquiry activity "Building Support for Play"). It is also crucial to help parents, administrators, and policymakers see that mandates that seek to increase individual children's test scores depend upon a 20th-century view of reading achievement (Meyer & Whitmore, 2011). This outdated perspective relies on "basics" that are remnants of print-based literacy in industrialized economies rather than digital economies where information is increasingly image- or video-based and can be instantly Googled. Early literacy education needs an updated set of basics (Dyson, 2006), informed by modern childhoods, children's diverse cultural resources, digital technologies (Vasquez & Felderman, 2012), and global media repertoires (Medina & Wohlwend, in press). Literacy 2.0 (Knobel & Wilber, 2009) represents a new way of thinking that moves away from the literacy 1.0 model of an individual interacting independently with a print text, whether in a book or onscreen. Literacy 2.0 represents the multiple ways of making meaning using the principles of web 2.0 interaction: global participation, multi-user collaboration, and distributed resources and knowledge.

We argue that a literacy 2.0 mind-set encompasses children's viewing, playing, and producing of digital popular media as well as daily interactions with the most ordinary transmedia products. The U.S. Department of Education recently recognized the educational potential of media texts by expanding its support of children's television viewing to include their interactions with transmedia. An evaluation of the Ready to Learn program identified the following benefits of including transmedia in early childhood education (U.S. Department of Education website, 2011):

- It presents children with multiple entry points to learning. Children can start learning via any one of the individual media, but when these media are interconnected, children will be motivated to explore even more;
- It enables educators to use individual media for the functions for which they are best suited. For example, games are particularly good problem-solving environments that encourage children to try difficult things without fear of failure; they are not as good as video, however, at presenting more linear and orderly information; and
- The rich, fictional worlds of transmedia tend to create a greater level of social interaction that can inspire children to create their own stories and media products and to share them with each other.

Conclusion

Literacy Playshop is a literacy 2.0 approach to early childhood literacy teaching, learning, and curriculum based on children's expertise and teachers' responsive mediation; the Literacy Playshops described in this book focus on play-based filmmaking with transmedia. This approach assumes a strength orientation to diversity and development (Volk & Long, 2005), which appreciates and integrates children's rich cultural repertoires (Gutiérrez & Rogoff, 2003) and family literacies and technologies (Vasquez & Felderman, 2012). The following chapters provide glimpses of early childhood classrooms where teachers encouraged popular media play and filmmaking as productive literacies that give children more equitable access to their diverse literacy resources.

CHAPTER 2

Media Processes in a K/1 Playshop

Beth A. Buchholz and Linda Skidmore Coggin

It's a Friday in early March and the gray Midwest winter is stubbornly extending its stay. Inside this warm and welcoming classroom, however, 50 kindergarten and 1st-grade students sit in a large circle excitedly eyeing their folders spread out on the floor. These are no ordinary schoolwork folders, but rather students' new storytelling folders. Storyboards and lined paper—recording tools from earlier workshops in this classroom—have been expanded to include character drawings, puppets on Popsicle sticks, and the early stages of set designs. Many of these artifacts have three-dimensional elements that poke out, refusing to be contained by a folder.

Doriet takes a seat in the circle and talks with students about that day's workshop. She chooses her words carefully, deliberately opening up new possibilities for peer engagement and what it means to write a story—suggesting that students may tell a story, play a story, make a story, enact a story: "Storytellers, yesterday you continued to work on storytelling, and some of you worked together, telling the same story. You're going to be invited to find your folder in just a minute and to find those collaborators, those people you are working with and sharing ideas with and continue to work on your story together."

Doriet's emphasis on collaborative meaning-making with an expanded set of tools complements and extends the literacy activities that students can engage in related to media and production. As is common in many elementary classrooms, writing workshop in Doriet and Elizabeth's K/1 multi-age classroom typically consisted of a teacher-led mini-lesson, independent writing time for students, and finally a whole-class sharing time. Conversation did naturally occur between students at tables spread throughout the room, but generally each student produced his or her own writing on paper using words and pictures. On this day, however, Doriet and Elizabeth worked to explicitly open up a broader sense of authorship possibilities and highlighted a range of potential tools for students to engage in the meaning-making process. In this new Literacy Playshop, the rules for composing had changed.

Doriet calls out the names written in large black letters on the folders, and students excitedly clamor toward the center of the circle to snatch their folders while looking for friends to work with. Small groups and partnerships begin to form around the room as children empty the objects from their folders and begin making authorly decisions together. Talk, laughter, and movement create a sense of energy in the room as students make stories together rather than write or plan stories independently.

In the back of the classroom, Liana and Janelle set up their two pieces of scenery on bookshelves in the library area. By putting the scenery on the top shelf the girls are able to sit on the floor and use the character puppets they've created. The characters start talking to one another in front of the scenery; however, eventually the story grows beyond the scene as the characters chase each other around in circles.

Liana and Janelle run circles around a group of boys on the floor who are focused on creating a three-dimensional ocean scene based on the book series Beast Quest. *Monroe started this work yesterday and today many friends have joined him to create the detailed features that are attached to the 2-foot-by-4-foot base that Monroe has created by taping many small pieces of paper together. The boys negotiate everything from what color to make the water to where to place the serpent to how many waves to put in a certain area.*

Across the room Amanda tries to convince the four girls in her group that they should move from the table to an open wall space where they can hang the scenery pieces to look like the backdrop of a play. [All children's names in the book are pseudonyms.]

Within this collaborative Literacy Playshop space, it is evident just how close the connection is between play and storying and how comfortable children are in this new space. Releasing students from the expectations of independent authorship and expanding the range of tools for making meaning provided *all* of the kindergarten and 1st-grade students with opportunities to access and share stories. The familiar complaint of "I don't know what to write about" was replaced with, "Ohhh, can we have more time?" as the playshop came to a close later that morning. This chapter provides an opportunity to observe young children's continued engagement in a Literacy Playshop as well as a chance to listen in on teachers' reflective conversations that reveal the tensions and questions that emerged throughout the curriculum development process.

An Emergent Literacy Play Curriculum

To understand this particular Friday in March and appreciate the proceeding curricular turn toward Literacy Playshop, it is important to consider the reflective process that Doriet and Elizabeth engaged in over the school year as part of a teacher study group focused on developing productive approaches to media literacy curriculum. These teachers were committed to thoughtful kidwatching, which constantly informed the curricula that emerged in this space around media production. Through daily conversation with one another and bimonthly study group meetings, Doriet and Elizabeth embarked on a journey *with* students to consider what it meant for young children to engage in a media production framework.

Months earlier, as winter break approached, Doriet and Elizabeth had loosely mapped out a media literacy curricular unit of study focused on popular media and production, which they planned to begin in January. Coming from a strong critical literacy paradigm, they planned for students to spend the first few weeks of the unit engaged in critical conversations and deconstruction work around popular media. Over the course of the 6 weeks that followed, they would then invite students to create their own media. Elizabeth and Doriet saw this unit unfolding across multiple parts of the school day, but to make space in an already busy classroom schedule, they decided that the bulk of their critical literacy teaching about popular media would be implemented during writing workshop. Their rationale was that by this point in the school year, writing workshop offered a comfortable framework for both students and teachers. However, from the beginning Doriet and Elizabeth recognized that it didn't have to be either writing workshop *or* Literacy Playshop–it could be writing workshop *and* Literacy Playshop.

As is evident by the preceding vignettes, this chapter isn't the success story of Doriet and Elizabeth's original plan. This is the success story of two teachers negotiating a truly emergent critical media literacy curriculum *with* students on a daily basis—a curriculum that ultimately surprised Elizabeth and Doriet and caused them to question some of the classroom structures they considered best practice. By the time the teacher study group met in early February, the teachers were reflecting on the emergent nature of this literacy approach with young children. There were no guidebooks, no set of instructions for how to support this unique classroom in engaging critically with popular media production. The teachers found curriculum development a discursive process where they were constantly asking questions such as:

- What does it mean for young children to engage critically with popular culture?
- How can we support students in producing meaningful media?
- What does the media production process look like?

Critical Conversations around Gender and Popular Media

The curricular journey with students began with a series of classroom conversations about heroes, villains, and power. Elizabeth and Doriet added pictures of different animated movie characters (e.g., Lightning McQueen, Mr. Incredible, Woody, Nemo) to each day of the large classroom calendar and asked students, "Are the characters on the calendar good or bad? How do you know?" This led to subsequent conversations guided by prompts such as:

- What makes a hero a hero?
- Can villains be boys or girls?
- Why do some people choose to be heroes and others villains?
- Who is a hero in your life?
- Can you be your own hero?

Conversations like these are situated in a traditional critical literacy paradigm, where children are expected to deconstruct popular media images and characters before producing their own media that "talk back" to (i.e., critique) the deconstructed texts. Elizabeth and Doriet's aim with these conversations was to help children recognize heroic qualities in everyday people, not just simply comic book or cartoon characters.

In late January, following the discussions about heroes, students viewed segments of the Disney Pixar film *Toy Story 3* (Unkrich, 2010). Many students were already familiar with the ongoing storyline of Woody, Buzz Lightyear, and Jessie through personal experiences with the *Toy Story* films and the wide range of popular products produced in connection with the films. As the highest-grossing film of 2010 and winner of the Academy Award for best animated feature, *Toy Story 3* was a deliberate choice by Doriet and Elizabeth to bring a popular media text into the classroom that most students' families already had a high level of comfort with. The decision to show film clips ensured that all students had equitable access to the text, to support students in engaging in critical conversations about the film's characters, storyline, and production—and eventually lead students into producing their own short films.

Elizabeth and Doriet posed the following prompt as part of the daily morning message written on an easel: "Write your name under one character you would like to be." Small laminated pictures of Woody, Buzz Lightyear, Jessie, Hamm (the piggy bank), Mr. Potato Head, and Barbie were taped below the prompt. Later that morning the students gathered in a large circle to discuss their character choices. The conversation fell along gendered lines—not surprising to experienced early childhood educators—with most of the boys choosing Buzz Lightyear and the girls divided between Jessie and Barbie. The boys' reasoning repeatedly cited what Buzz could "do," his various "cool" parts, and the funny things he said in the movie. The girls' talk focused on Jessie and Barbie being characters who were pretty, "stuck with their friends," and "took care" of others. In general, the children's rationales aligned with prevalent themes identified in cultural studies of consumption and children's media masculinities that value action and technology and femininities that value relationships and nurture (Orr, 2009; Willett, 2008). The aim of conversations such as these was to help students deconstruct characters, yet the students' choices and rationales regarding characters remained tightly constricted by stereotypical gender norms.

Sensing that this conversation was not going in the direction she hoped, Elizabeth tried moving in a more critical direction by inviting students to consider what *Toy Story 3* character they would want to be friends with. She continued, "Would you choose a friend based on what they look like? What they can do? Or would you choose a friend based on how they made you feel?" This discussion resumed the following school day with a final question about what character in the movie students felt was most like them. Conversation was again rooted in students' gendered identities as Ida offered that she was most like Barbie "because she's pretty and wants to be with friends," while Thomas selected Buzz Lightyear since "he was doing funny stuff."

In a teacher study group meeting a few days later, both Elizabeth and Doriet expressed frustration over the inability of questions like these to lead students into rich conversations around popular media. They had clear ideas of what it would sound like for students to be critical media consumers. However, they felt they hadn't hit upon the "magic, just right question" that would invite children into a critical space around these beloved films and characters. They also wondered if their own biases and agendas were embedded in their questions.

An additional activity that Doriet and Elizabeth designed to encourage critical conversations involved students sorting a large group of McDonald's Happy Meal media toys into "boy" and "girl" piles. Doriet took a picture of the sorted piles and the following day students were given a copy of this photograph and invited to work in small groups to talk about and record what they noticed about the different piles. Although two students, Monroe and Ian, tried suggesting that there "was no such thing as boys' and girls' toys," most of the students did not critique the toys in ways that Elizabeth and Doriet had hoped. Most groups circled the toys they liked, gave numerical observations, or labeled the different toys. Elizabeth expressed tensions related to these types of critical media literacy activities and conversations, reflecting that it often felt like teachers were "pushing [their] own agenda onto kids." She also questioned whether students who offered a critical perspective, like Ian and Monroe, were simply engaged in teacher-pleasing. Elizabeth and Doriet had hoped to support children in becoming discerning consumers of popular media characters and storylines, but found that most students were unable to separate themselves from the movies, characters, and toys they were so passionately attached to.

In light of these tensions around these critical literacy activities, Doriet and Elizabeth began to reconsider what it would mean for their young students to be critical. Rather than continuing to search for the "right question" that would lead students into talking about media, they decided to move forward with activities that engaged students in producing media. This change in direction was the result of Elizabeth and Doriet's concerns regarding students' abilities to engage in critical conversation around popular media, and Karen's (Wohlwend) comment in a study group meeting that "maybe it's not a question" that will lead to critical experiences for kids, "maybe [they] have to play it to feel it." (Throughout the book the name *Karen* refers to one of the preschool teachers unless otherwise noted, as above.)

Play: Positioning Children as Storytellers

The theme of "playing it" began to take shape one morning in early February as Elizabeth invited students to draw toys and characters. With white paper, colored pencils, and markers scattered around, students eagerly drew both original and popular media characters. Amanda worked on a horse named Maley with a detailed bridle, Samuel created "SiCLOPaS" [Cyclops], and Kaley drew Woody from *Toy Story 3*. Conversation filled the room as students excitedly discussed characters with one another. Maxwell even took on the voice of his character as he shared ideas with Arthur across the small table. One student's simple request at the end of this workshop time—"Can I cut out my character?"—pushed this activity even further over the next few days and served as a sort of turning point in the ways Doriet and Elizabeth began to understand children's work with popular media.

Cutting out the characters and toys that students had drawn changed the way they interpreted what they were doing. It moved the activity from a school-based writing/drawing activity into a play-based activity that naturally positioned children as storytellers. Cutting out the characters made them more than just drawings on a page; they were now dolls and action figures to be manipulated and in desperate need of stories. During these workshops, children's writing, drawing, playing, and storytelling became inseparable from one another. Students worked on these characters for multiple days, and Elizabeth's directions at the start of the workshop moved from simply inviting children to draw characters to suggesting that children "think about the story you're creating" and use some of the workshop time to "tell a story with your cut-out toys." This process of making characters and playing stories was recursive for children: students would construct characters, tell stories, make new characters, revise the previous story, and so on. Many students even began creating scenery and props related to the stories they were composing. These workshops were the earliest moments of what would weeks later become the basis for a more sustained Literacy Playshop. Elizabeth identified this work as "one of the best parts of the week" because the experience was "so rich" and "so revealing." The power of play in the storying process was evident, but for the next few weeks the characters stayed in students' storytelling folders as Doriet, Elizabeth, and the students headed into the serious work of creating storyboards.

Storying: Representing Film on Paper with Storyboards

Doriet and Elizabeth viewed storyboards as an integral tool in the planning phase of the film production process, which they saw aligning closely with the writing process that students were already familiar with in writing workshop: brainstorm, plan, draft, write, revise, edit, and publish. Video cameras would be introduced to students after they used words and/or pictures to map out a complete story on paper. Elizabeth and Doriet had experimented with storyboards as a planning tool during the fall teacher study group meetings and were excited to introduce this new tool to students. The structure of storyboards offered teachers a sense of reassurance that the kindergarten and 1st-grade state reading and language arts standards were being covered as part of this emerging critical media curricula. For example, Doriet and Elizabeth were able to incorporate standards-based instruction on sequencing, characterization, story structure, and setting through-out their work with storyboards and storytelling. Even though Doriet and Eliza-beth initially saw this planning time as students getting one step closer to actual film production, they later came to question whether students understood this process in the same way, which ultimately led them to an expanded vision of au-thorship in the context of this unit.

Storyboards: An Integral Planning Tool for Film? A series of thought-ful whole-group, guided engagements were planned so that students could gain experience with storyboards. The Pixar short *The Adventures of André & Wally B* (Lasseter, 1984) was used to build students' familiarity with storyboards, and as Elizabeth noted it "took pressure off students [initially] having to generate their own stories." The 2-minute, humorous Pixar short involves a character named André waking up in a forest next to a bee named Wally B. Despite his efforts to get away, André is stung by Wally B but eventually gets the last laugh when Wally B is hit by André's hat. Selecting Pixar films such as *Toy Story 3* and *The Adventures of André & Wally B* reflected teachers' careful decision-making throughout the cur-ricular development process to bring "safe" mainstream media into the classroom that they anticipated would receive little resistance from students' families.

After watching the film, Doriet introduced a way to retell the story using a six-block storyboard. She talked with students about some of the difficulties in translating the three-dimensional action of film onto a two-dimensional piece of paper. The limitations of representing action on a storyboard would be something that students and teachers would continue to experiment with over the course of the unit. Students took clipboards and spread out around the room to indepen-dently work on their André and Wally B storyboards.

The following day Doriet replayed *The Adventures of André & Wally B*, watch-ing 20-second clips to discuss with the children what they noticed and how they might go about analyzing the film. Doriet reminded the children to reflect on the storyboards they had worked on the previous day and to consider if they had left out any important events. Later students were given time to continue working on these storyboards. Even though the storyboard included blank lines for recording words underneath each box, almost all of the children used only pictures to rep-resent the film. Doriet and Elizabeth did not pressure students to include words at this early stage. This is remarkable because the emphasis on writing words has become increasingly intense in even the earliest grades due to the skills mastery discourse instantiated in state and national standards (Wohlwend, 2009). Story-boards offered these children an opportunity to envision multiple ways of writing a story, and this notion of writing would be expanded even further during the unit.

In addition to working with popular media and production, this story-boarding activity required that students engage in comprehension strategies such as determining importance and synthesizing, which are routinely taught in reading instruction at all grade levels. In contrast to many classrooms where texts are limited to books, in this classroom, popular media such as film allowed children to develop comprehension strategies in relation to the texts they encounter beyond school.

After a few days of creating storyboards based on multiple Pixar shorts, students were invited to create original storyboards. Following a writing workshop structure, teachers developed mini-lessons related to storyboards, often modeling and thinking aloud about the process of recording a story in your head on paper. Wordless picture books by David Wiesner were also introduced as mentor texts to highlight illustration techniques and sequencing concepts that children were encouraged to incorporate into their storyboards. At the conclusion of each mini-lesson, students grabbed storytelling folders and worked independently on their own storyboards. Students had complete choice in the stories and topics they chose to include in their storyboards, which allowed students to pull from well-known cultural and popular media resources.

Monroe, a lively and imaginative storyteller, lies on his stomach, leans on his left elbow, and rifles through his storytelling folder to find the storyboard he started working on the day before. As he's reading, thinking, and then considering what might happen next in his Star Wars-inspired lightsaber duel between Darth Vader and an unnamed opponent, he casually asks Liana, who's sitting nearby, what she's writing about. She seems a little surprised to be asked, but replies that she's writing about "a kitten … and stuff." Monroe explains that he's writing a hilarious comic, then qualifies that he's at least "trying to make it hilarious."

Staring at the empty sixth square, Monroe grabs a pencil and writes, "tHey Die." [See Figure 2.1 for his storyboard.] Before moving on to add the picture, though, he rereads what he has just written and quietly adds a question mark to the end, thus (possibly) prolonging Darth Vader's life and ultimately prolonging the life of the story onto a second storyboarding sheet. He eagerly gets another piece of storyboarding paper. Staring at the blank sheet, Monroe admits to everyone sitting nearby that he's now "wondering what should come next." What he eventually decides is, "WELL YA tHEY DO DIE"; this trick ending makes Monroe laugh each time as he rereads it. Once this concluding scene is drawn, he jumps up, seeking an audience to share his story with. Moving around the room, he searches for friends to read his piece aloud to, each time laughing at his surprise ending.

It is worth emphasizing that Monroe did not run over to share his piece with Doriet or Elizabeth—rather, he sought out a *peer* audience. Monroe's actions reveal the deep longing of an author wanting to share something that matters with people who matter. Writing workshop advocates emphasize the importance of a daily share time that offers children authentic, peer-based feedback throughout the writing process (Calkins, 1994). Monroe's engagement in the writing process and pride in his writing are surely what all teachers hope for when they envision authorship in the early childhood classroom. Storyboard work did seem to tap into students' energy, something that had been lacking during the previous week's

Figure 2.1. Monroe's Storyboard with Original Ending

talk about film. But as the days progressed, even Monroe's enthusiasm waned at the prospect of creating *another* storyboard. In fact, he later complained that he "didn't know what to write about." How is it possible that such an imaginative storyteller went from being completely engaged to having nothing to write about?

The Limitations of Storyboards. Doriet and Elizabeth were quick to pick up on the behaviors of Monroe and other students who appeared to lose steam with the storyboarding process. At first, they assumed students were struggling for *ideas.* In response, Doriet introduced a heart-mapping invitation as a brainstorming strategy (Heard, 1998). Each student drew a large heart on a piece of paper and filled it with pictures and words that described things that "filled [his/her] heart" (e.g., family, friends, sports and other activities, toys). Doriet explained to students that writers "often get stuck" and demonstrated how she could use her own heart map to help come up with a new storyboard idea. Despite Doriet's explicit modeling on how to take an idea from a heart map and stretch it across a storyboard, teachers still had the sense that children were stuck.

A teacher study group soon after provided the time and space for teachers to think in depth about this sense of feeling stuck with storyboarding as a step in the media production process. Doriet noted that one of the main issues was how challenging it seemed to be for students to "take film and play and [try] to translate that in and out of writing." She brought up the playful storytelling atmosphere that had erupted in the room a few weeks earlier when children were invited to create and cut toys out of paper. In this instance, children took on character voices, actions, and complex dialogue, which produced rich moments of storytelling that were much deeper than what children were now representing on storyboards. Specifically, the teachers used Monroe as an example of a student who had "elaborate stories that are lost" in the transduction to paper. Elizabeth now believed that it wasn't that Monroe was at a loss for ideas; it was that he was frustrated with being unable to represent his ideas fully on paper. Rather than finding the storyboard a useful planning tool, teachers wondered if it limited the range and complexity of stories students were producing.

Teachers also questioned whether students even understood that the storyboards were a planning tool for film. Although film had been a significant part of the curriculum in terms of viewings and conversations, students had not been explicitly told that they would be making a film or been introduced to the potential new tool, video cameras. Elizabeth wondered if this was the "missing piece" that was contributing to the sense that storyboards seemed "not to go anywhere." The storyboards (disconnected from film) were simply inviting students to use the same tools and routines from writing workshop; complex live-action stories still had to be simplified into versions that could be represented on paper. With these issues in mind, Doriet and Elizabeth worked together to map out a new curricular trajectory that highlighted play and a set of new tools as critical components of the composing process and film production.

During another study group meeting, teachers discussed the best way to immediately introduce video cameras into the classroom. Doriet and Elizabeth considered using cameras as part of whole-class meetings that occurred at the end of the school day. In these meetings students directed small skits that reenacted social issues that had recently arisen in the classroom. Through these dramas, teachers facilitated conversations aimed at promoting children's social problem-solving skills. The teachers could see how adding a cameraperson to this role-playing structure seemed like a natural way to begin giving children experiences with the video camera. Adding a single camera to this whole-group structure could afford teachers a great deal of control in the learning process and allow them to model and talk through technical issues related to the camera with the whole group before letting small groups use the cameras more independently. This whole-class structure might also give students opportunities for more guided practice with the expert teacher positioned to step in as needed.

On the other hand, they could also see benefits to an entirely different approach: simply putting cameras into students' hands and saying, "Here's a tool for you to record your story. How could you use it?" Teachers in any grade can identify with the tension between thoughtfully scaffolded and planned lessons versus the (often messy) experiential learning process of trial-and-error discovery.

As Elizabeth and Doriet negotiated this tension, they began to revise some of their own beliefs about the structure and routines of writing workshop and how it fit into the world of new literacies and film production with young children.

An Expanded Vision of Authorship. Comparing the natural eruption of storytelling and playful collaboration when children were creating toys to the "stuck" feeling that teachers and students were experiencing with storyboarding caused Doriet and Elizabeth to question the basic structure of writing workshop as conceptualized in their classroom:

- Does every child need to create his/her own story (or in this case, storyboard)?
- Should a draft (storyboard) be required before publishing (filming) begins?
- Could some students skip writing altogether and take on different roles in the storytelling and filmmaking processes that speak to their personal strengths?

In the study group meeting, Doriet added that she and Elizabeth were considering these questions "especially in relation to writing workshop . . . [where] each student is being held accountable for independent work" and wondering what accountability might look like "with a collaborative effort." Doriet and Elizabeth admitted that they hadn't been able to settle on any definite answers, but Elizabeth emphasized, "it's definitely *the thing* we're thinking about."

It's helpful here to situate this discussion in a paradigm shift in literacy—from a standards-based, print-privileged school literacy paradigm to a media-resourced, new literacies paradigm. In traditional views of authorship, a writer works alone—assisted by peers and teachers—and progresses toward the adult model of independent, creative production. Juxtapose that with a new literacies paradigm like filmmaking, where collaborative, collective meaning-making experiences are emphasized and improvisation and connectivity are valued more than individual production (Knobel & Wilber, 2009; Marsh, 2009; Wohlwend, 2010). In the new literacies paradigm, it's not how much an individual knows, but how quickly he or she can access information, remix it, and share it. Individual accountability doesn't fit as well with new media projects as it does with the traditional image of the solitary author. In filmmaking, for example, a single person isn't expected to produce a film; collaboration among diverse roles (e.g., writers, directors, actors, editors, musicians) must be coordinated so that the text that is produced is greater than any one person or role.

During study group, Karen (Wohlwend) noted that authorship in this new literacies world is in a dramatic moment of shift from the independent to the collective and interactive. This means that teachers must also rethink traditional best practices in the classroom. Elizabeth and Doriet were immediately attracted to this view of collective authorship because it mirrored the "focus on a classroom community" that they worked so hard to build with the children across other parts of the school day. Whole-class meetings, group work, and teacher talk continually emphasized that "we're greater together than we are alone." Doriet and Elizabeth wondered whether this type of community work was reflected in the current configuration of writing workshop.

Entering this new terrain of collective authorship and filmmaking, Doriet and Elizabeth were excited but realistic about how "messy" they anticipated the process to be. They developed a tentative plan to have students wrap up their independent storyboards and to then introduce the Literacy Playshop structure to open up a composing environment where choice in tools figured prominently. Rather than a requirement, storyboards became one of many planning tools—scripts, play, sets, puppets, props, and costumes—the young filmmakers and storytellers could use to hold the meaning of a story. Teachers wanted students to use storyboards only "if it's a tool that makes sense." As teachers discussed how the Literacy Playshop would unfold in the classroom, they emphasized the importance of openness and choice. As one teacher noted, "Kids should choose a tool that makes the most sense for how they want to tell their story. Here are your tools. You want to record your film. What do you need from us?"

As teachers and students moved into Literacy Playshop, there was a sense of possibility that filled the room with energy and released stories from the two-dimensional confines of paper. But it was careful and diligent kidwatching that helped Elizabeth and Doriet plan the just-in-time mediation that sustained the Playshop over the following weeks and ensured that all of their students were growing as storytellers, collaborators, and media producers.

Production: Exploring New Ways to Make Meaning

A sign for parents and visitors just outside the classroom door only hinted at the activity inside: Storytelling and Filmmaking. Storytellers were creating their own characters and sets, casting actors and directing scenes, and sharing storytelling strategies with each other. Just a few days ago, students were writing on storyboard paper to capture a Pixar short film clip or to imagine a new story for favorite movie characters. In Literacy Playshop, scenes emerged from flat white paper and characters, supported by masking tape and Popsicle sticks, moved across the freshly inked landscapes. Children's voices mimicked characters from favorite movies, interspersed with talk that admonished, "you have to push the red button" to capture these new ways of composing story. As students moved beyond using storyboards as tools to record their story, other ways of making the story durable became evident. Amanda reminded Elizabeth, "What is on my storyboard is not the 'real' story. It is not telling the story, just showing what is happening." Similar to Monroe's struggle to draw the complexity of the story he envisioned, Amanda had realized that filmmaking involves more than can be recorded on a piece of paper by emergent writers.

The schedule as well as the physical space of this classroom were transformed to encompass these complexities as students engaged in filmmaking. Each day as the whole class gathered on the carpet in front of the screen at the beginning of the Literacy Playshop, Doriet and Elizabeth no longer modeled writing possibilities or procedures on chart paper as they had been doing. Students *and* teachers were now watching and analyzing the students' own explorations as filmmakers. The children were repositioned as knowledgeable critics as their films took center stage. This cycle of producing and sharing films allowed the children to draw on their own expertise as media consumers *and* producers as the class discussed problems, processes, and products that resulted from their explorations.

During these screenings, children collaboratively negotiated the "how-to's" of filmmaking, opening space to recognize children's popular media passions as valuable literacy resources and for diverse learners to perform literate identities. The first screening was a puppet show by Luis and Eden. The role of expert was new to Luis, who was often outside of the classroom working with another adult in remedial interventions. Luis is one of the "all" children—that is, children referred to in statements like "All children can learn" and "No child left behind" (Dyson, 2003b). He is not middle-class, white, or regularly successful in social or academic school tasks. However, his presence and engagement during his film's screening positioned him as a successful writer with valued expertise in this new medium. Participating in viewing and critical reflection of a collaboratively produced student film provided a rich entry point for Luis and other students, who were able to integrate their cultural repertoires and everyday literacies.

After a beginning discussion of what makes a good movie, Doriet stopped the video to ask, "What do you notice?" One girl noted that only Eden was "in the story" (visible in the camera frame). Another girl suggested that Doriet "replay" the scene "if some of you didn't see," highlighting conventions of this new way of recording a story. Teachers and students posed further questions and considered solutions to the problem, "How do you know what is in the camera frame?" The class discussions addressed parts of the movie where only one of the boys could be seen on camera: "How can you make sure that you are filming what you want?" "Did you mean for that to happen, Luis?" When it became clear that Luis didn't know that he was out of the frame, the questions then focused on problem-solving: "How could you take care of that?" As Luis and his fellow filmmakers brainstormed solutions, he was clearly taking on a new role of contributor in class discussion as an action filmmaker as he invested in exploring possible solutions. At first Luis said he would "wait a minute" and then go check (looking in the camera viewer) to see if he was still in the frame. Suddenly he exclaimed, "Wait! That doesn't make any sense!" when he realized that he couldn't be acting on screen and behind the camera at the same time.

Doriet and Elizabeth continued to position these young filmmakers as media producers able to consider a range of production decisions. When Doriet asked, "What are some other ways to solve this problem [of who is in the camera view]?", one child suggested that someone else stand behind the camera. In a just-in-time mediation, Doriet explained that this would be the "cameraperson." Similar decisions spontaneously made by young filmmakers during production were made visible during group viewings and opened up questions of production conventions as well as renegotiations of peer social relationships, such as: How do you decide who will be the actor and who will be the cameraperson? How do you make the setting of the story clear to viewers? The emerging media production framework and viewing of student-made films encouraged students to further explore solutions during Literacy Playshop as the connection between play, storying, collaboration, and production "played" out.

The multiple ways students think and make meaning together during the Playshop were evident in the varied storytelling styles and co-authoring literacy practices that students took up as filmmakers. After viewing one or two films produced during the previous Literacy Playshop, students used exploration and production time to play their emerging knowledge of filmmaking as a key literacy activity. As students created scenery, puppets, and props, these materials for enacting characters and settings became new composition tools for anchoring story meanings.

Some groups of students explored how to tape background scenes to tables to create a continuous background for filming while others propped up storytelling folders and filmed "close up" to the scene. Students' imaginative thinking was evident as the classroom's blue carpet became the ocean and pipe cleaners were transformed into wedding rings. Filmmaking afforded new possibilities for establishing character traits and actions that transformed the flat figures drawn on storyboards. Students explored characters' physical actions and voice qualities, sound effects, and camera angles, which added another dimension to their storytelling.

Students improvised on the story (sometimes originally conceived and recorded on a storyboard) during dramatic play. As filming proceeded, characters from popular texts or students' own stories became characters in a different story as students frequently stopped the action to negotiate character moves or voices, revealing the momentary nature of the collaborative meaning-making. Children also explored using cameras in multiple ways. Occasionally cameras became recorders for sound effects or pretend cell phones, or were used to "just pretend" to make a film. In just-in-time mediations in response to viewing films and productive kidwatching, Elizabeth asked the students to consider size (of puppets, props, or scenery) in relation to the camera frame. She wondered, How is the camera going to capture the character or scene? Explorations with cameras occurred both away from and during film production, revealing how children played together to learn about and produce media.

With camera in hand, Ida positions her face in front of a research video camera. "Can you see me?" she asks and directs Cane to "please step back."

*   "I don't have to!"*

Cane wiggles his fingers in front of the camera to see how this works and Ida joins him.
"Not too close," he says.

"I know," Ida replies. Suddenly Ida pops up in front of the camera saying, "Introduce me!"

At another table in the middle of the busy K/1 classroom, two girls are using the video camera to make a "pretend" video. One of the girls, Ellen, is not recording but narrating her story, using the camera as if it were a microphone. She reappropriates Toy Story characters, Woody and Bullseye, in her story.

Ellen directs her partner, Kaley, "Bring Bullseye here!" and Kaley positions the Bullseye paper puppet in front of Ellen's camera.

"Here's Bullseye!" Ellen narrates as she turns on the camera. "Get Woody. What the heck?" Ellen wonders as she turns the camera sideways to "film" Woody. A child from a neighboring film group inquires whether Ellen's camera is on. Examining the camera, Ellen flips the "on" button (not the record button), turns to Kaley, and says, "Let's start over" as she begins "filming" again.

Collaboration: Transforming Meanings Together

Doriet and Elizabeth reflected on the ways that collaboration opened up entry points for the storying process. In one study group session, Doriet recalled, "I think reflecting back what was most interesting was kids who were struggling to write or think of a story, when they were able to collaborate, I think, felt more confident and more a part of the story. [It wasn't only the process that transformed but] what story looked like shifted" within this collaborative process.

As students continued to use live action or puppets to create films, teachers designed engagements that foregrounded the collaborative process of storying. One of these whole-group guided engagements resulted in a collaboratively played story about Bellybutton, a kangaroo heroine in a Snow White variant invented by the children. Students gathered for several days to compose and enact the story together. On one particular day, Doriet began the collaborative time guiding students to remember "what we've agreed on about the story so far," emphasizing the collaborative nature of this storytelling. As student actors took roles as Bellybutton, a barn, and trees, students recalled and acted the story's beginning actions and offered suggestions for what might happen next in the story.

Familiar story elements and characters from children's favorite popular media permeated this "writing." This story repeated the damsel-in-distress scenario from Disney Princess films—embodied by the new heroine, Bellybutton. However, as students sat knee-to-knee to brainstorm what might happen next, a group of boys proposed Darth Vader, a central character and antagonist of the *Star Wars* movies, as a likely character to bring a poison apple. Teachers chose to disrupt the gendered storyline by opening the possibility of substituting a *Star Wars* villain for the evil queen, a move that required negotiation and improvisation to reconcile the two narratives. The challenge of making the boys' idea make sense within the story was negotiated by all class members in the next whole-group playing.

The next day, as the class gathered to replay this collaborative story, Doriet foregrounded the collaborative process by saying that a "variety of ideas to change the story [are needed] as we build it. We look as the story unfolds, step back, and make changes. We are all directors." Several student directors shared ideas for what the narrator could say to introduce Darth Vader into the scene. This engagement became a model for critical collaboration as this played text demonstrated the emergent nature of the storying process and the power of collaboration to challenge expected gender boundaries and negotiate shared meanings (Marsh, 2006; Wohlwend, 2011).

Four Processes: Playing, Storying, Collaborating, and Producing

Playing, collaborating, storying, and producing are not isolated processes in the Literacy Playshop. One group originally recorded their story on several pages of storyboard paper. Cane, the only boy in this group, created a list of characters to record who would play each role, much like the credits at the end of a movie. The story emerged from Cane's cast list as the group negotiated the story's content in the process of play and production. Other groups used the Playshop space to leave the storyboard behind and reimagine their story with three-dimensional materials. One child created an elaborate paper mask and costume pieces but quickly shed his costume and actor's role to take up a camera to film friends working on the large set. These scenarios and the following vignette illustrate the dynamic processes of a literacy play curriculum forged as teachers and students shared the lead.

After several days, a group continues to discuss "finishing" the scenery they are creating for their film. As they remove paper backgrounds and character puppets from storytelling folders, three children in this large all-girl film-making group begin taping scenes around a table, negotiating where to put each one and which character they will play today. Liana confidently asserts, "Okay, I'll be the lady," as she looks through the puppets on the table. The other girls are immersed in the set they are designing.

After a couple of minutes, Ida, the chosen cameraperson, looks into the research camera to announce, "Starting in a minute." Two of the girls get under the table with their puppets, a position they already tried on another day to ensure that the puppets would be in front of the scenery and that their own bodies would not obstruct the camera view. The girls continue to discuss what they will be doing "during the show" as they set up.

Simone, another group member, has moved her background scene from around the table and taped it to the back of a chair. She crouches behind the slim chair back and can easily wrap her arms around to the front to manipulate the pink and blue spotted dog she has affixed to Popsicle sticks she holds in each hand. Another group member, Ladonna, watches this new plan intently as Ida films the scene.

Even when filming stops, Simone continues to move the puppet. She has taken on the position of audience member as well as actor as she looks over the chair back and gazes intently at the scene she is creating. As the real filmmaking begins, Simone quickly removes her part of the scene from the chair back where she has been rehearsing to include it in the group's scene. The other girls move in and out from under the table, and the cameraperson seeks adult help to make sure she is recording.

"Go!" Liana announces, "and illustrated by Simone, Jenna, and Ida, and the rest" as she nervously fidgets with her shirt. "Please enjoy the show!"

The action pauses as Ladonna quickly clears the table of the storytelling folders and loose papers that remain. The other girls rush to get their puppets and retape a portion of the scenery that has fallen as they crawled in and out from under the table. Ida continues. "Wait! I didn't start it [the recording]. Start over, start over, start over… So get in your poses, get in your poses, get in your poses!"

The girls with puppets begin moving their characters around in front of the scenery, arms extended so the camera can "see" them as Ida starts to record.

Another camera problem pauses the action again. But this time Ida solves it on her own and announces that she is turning the camera back on, so "get in your poses really fast. Are you ready?"

As the four characters begin again, Ladonna lays down her puppet to readjust the scenery, Liana and Julie act, and Ida moves in closer to film the action. The girls spontaneously dialogue in character as they occasionally look at each other and then back on their own puppets.

Suddenly Ida announces, "It's my part [in the movie] now. Someone take my spot!"

Liana shouts, "I'll take it," as she and Ladonna grab for the camera at the same time.

"Thank you!" Ida hands the camera to Ladonna, and Liana resumes her part, seemingly undaunted by her failure to assume the coveted position of cameraperson. Ida searches for her character and the other girls continue to act in character as Ladonna begins filming. Ida soon returns with her puppet character, which has "Ida" written in orange marker across its body, and joins the action.

In this Literacy Playshop example, these young producers negotiated their way through complex play and storytelling decisions during the film production. The collaboration resulted in a played text that held some resemblance to the written storyboard they created weeks ago, as the actors moved in and out of roles as set designer, actor, technical advisor, and cameraperson. Desirable roles were anchored by cameras or puppets; whoever held the camera could take up the role of cameraperson with the authority to direct other children. Similarly, Ida's name on her horse marked the puppet as her property but also secured her role and participation in the film. Children composed within this play space as they drew upon familiar and original storylines and characters, which shaped experience and understanding of literacies and their own identities as multimodal literacy users and media producers.

These are not classroom scenes typically associated with writing in an early childhood classroom. During study group sessions, Karen (Wohlwend) and the teachers discussed how video work inspires action rehearsal in contrast to verbal rehearsals in drafting, conferring, and revising in the writing process. The young filmmakers played their way through the complex thinking and action of the process of filming meanings that did not translate to paper. Just as children found active filmmaking processes that gave new forms of expression to their elaborate storylines, teachers experienced tensions and successes in negotiating new forms of literacy in partnership with children.

A Film Festival Focused on Process

It is late April and the smell of popcorn fills the K/1 room classroom as students' parents and younger siblings wander in looking for seats. Invitations sent home to each family promised that today's film festival would be a celebration of students' work related to media, storytelling, and film over the last few months. Students sit clustered on the carpet facing the large screen and nervously awaiting the official start of the festival. They whisper among themselves, wondering what the groups will share today and perhaps more important wondering when the popcorn will be handed out—after all, what film viewing event is complete without popcorn? Doriet welcomes the families to the event and explains that the students have a wide variety of films and live action performances to share. With that, the lights dim and the sharing begins.

In writing workshop, a celebration such as this offers an opportunity for students to share polished pieces of writing with a larger audience. Teachers often feel pressure during these types of events to have students share only pieces that have been through the revision, editing, and publication steps of the writing process, perhaps assuming that parents expect to see finished products. Teachers who have hosted writing celebrations know the stress of trying to get an entire classroom of students to publish a piece of writing by a certain day. It can often feel like this publishing step is more work for the teacher than the students. Doriet and Elizabeth understood how difficult it would be for students to have final, polished films ready by the end of April, but they wanted to bring closure to the unit and share some of the students' remarkable work. Rather than follow the natural urge to take over parts of the production process to ensure that all students had a polished film, Doriet and Elizabeth encouraged children to present their most current work at the film festival. Children chose to share everything from rough drafts of storyboards to live action dramas to recorded films. The range of products on display invited families to get a glimpse of the diverse tools that the students used throughout the literacy play curriculum.

The resulting storytelling products shared at the K/1 film festival reflected Doriet and Elizabeth's extraordinary ability to let go of publishing as a *final* product and instead showcase works in progress that documented the different processes and ways to write discovered in the playshop. One of Elizabeth's major takeaways from the storytelling and film production phase was how "the constraints of different parts of the filmmaking process [i.e., story patterns, types of camera shots] actually opened things up for children in different ways." This opening up of student expression was reflected in the variety of products shared at the festival:

- Telling the story in film through live action
- Using puppets or other props and acting
- Walking through an elaborate set creation
- Collaborating and acting out another student's narration of the story
- Reading and showing the storyboard as a written story

Some groups chose to link separate films that were labeled "Part 1," "Part 2," and "Part 3," allowing for more individual expression within a cohesive whole. One group of young actors improvised when faced with the absence of the primary character in their live-action play. They renegotiated roles and action to produce the story live, relishing in the instant feedback provided by the eager audience of parents, siblings, and peers. These performances reflected the many forms of playing, collaborating, and storying that emerged as teachers and students worked in tandem to engage in meaningful media production.

Conclusion

The Literacy Playshop developed as a result of collaborative meaning-making where children could *think and act* in the multiple modalities of film and play. Elizabeth and Doriet's commitment to thoughtful kidwatching enabled them to uncover what it means for young children to engage critically in a media-rich literacy play curriculum. Intertwining processes of play, collaboration, storying, and production transformed the classroom into a Literacy Playshop that:

- Celebrated played texts that grew out of collaboration and negotiation among peers
- Expanded storyboards from a tool of writing to include paper settings, embodied characters, and popular storylines and negotiated action
- Opened up space for all kinds of writers

Not only did processes of writing stories change, but what storying looked like changed in the process.

CHAPTER 3

Mediation Levels in a Preschool Playshop

Christy Wessel Powell and Nicholas E. Husbye

Taylor steps into view of the camera, his head wrapped by a black bandanna and a construction-paper mustache below his nose. He paces for a moment before Sara, one of his teachers, whispers, "Say it loud, Taylor: the pirates are coming!" Taylor stops pacing, turns to his classmates, and bellows, "The pirates are coming!" before climbing the stairs to the classroom loft, which serves as the pirate ship. A line of classmates follow him onto the loft platform as Taylor commands, "Set sail!"

Thus began the final dress rehearsal for *The Pirate Movie*, a project in which 20 preschool children and their teachers, Sara and Karen, had invested much time and energy. Over the course of the 45-minute rehearsal, the preschoolers—with help from their teachers—worked through a collaboratively drafted storyline. They occasionally changed their story in the moments when Karen and Sara questioned them about their characters' reactions as the story was played out in physical space. These questions and the children's chorused responses served to expand and stabilize the story, connecting and making sense of the clusters of actions the students had decided upon in the planning stages of the movie.

This chapter describes the levels of mediation that surrounded media production in the preschool Literacy Playshop, detailing the ways that filmmaking aligned with the structured and unstructured play that children engaged every day. We describe how filmmaking unfolded in two preschool classrooms as teachers mediated children's play and media storytelling in a variety of productive and supportive ways, from 1) guided engagements that co-constructed *The Pirate Movie* to 2) "just-enough" mediation and "just-in-time" teaching with puppets or storyboards to 3) moments of independent and exploratory play in classroom centers. First, we return to the guided production of a whole-group film in Karen and Sara's classroom of 3- to 5-year-old children.

The preschoolers encounter a shark and a sea monster. Adrift on a sea of carpet with only their cardboard dinghies, the pirates pause and look toward Sara and Karen. Sara prompts, "Okay, we need to figure out whether they are friendly or if they are mean. How do we find out?"

"Ask them!" chime the preschoolers.

"Okay, who's going to ask them?" coaches Sara.

"I will," a child's voice answers.

"Okay, ask them, 'Are you friendly, shark and sea monster?' "

The pirate echoes Sara's words and the shark whispers, "I'm friendly."

Sara, not hearing this, repeats the question as a prompt, "Are you friendly?"

Both the children playing the shark and the sea monster smile.

"Yes, you're friendly. You're smiling!" Sara says to the aquatic duo.

"I said," the shark replies, "that I was friendly!"

Having determined that the shark and the sea monster are friendly, the pirates scoot along the carpeted floor in their cardboard dinghies, returning to their ship. There is, after all, treasure to be found.

This scene is but a small moment in the process of creating *The Pirate Movie*. Over several weeks, Sara and Karen guided students through the filmmaking process and negotiated with the children to create co-constructed lists of characters, props, dialogue, and an action sequence. In both preschool classrooms, filmmaking posed an occasionally rewarding and often challenging task for the teachers and children: rewarding in the ways that capturing and comparing filmed episodes of play at various times helped teachers understand and mediate children's meaning-making development, and challenging in the anchoring of meanings and navigation of a fluid storytelling that shifted with the interests of the children in the classroom. In a way, it was as though the teachers had encountered their very own sea monster and shark in the form of filmmaking in the preschool classroom. It is an encounter that begs the question: Is it possible to make the tools and processes of filmmaking friendly to a negotiated, developmentally appropriate, and emergent curriculum in a child-centered classroom?

Taking their cue from the children, Sara and Karen "ask them," of course. They teach in one of two preschool classrooms in a university child care center. Both classrooms are bright, airy spaces filled with the wooden furniture, cubbies, and tubs brimming with materials of early childhood education: books, paints, water, and sand. Sara and Karen, with Dawn and Michiru, their colleagues in the other classroom, are thoughtful, careful, and deliberate educators, grounded by collective beliefs in early childhood education that honor children's experiences and align with professional discourse about developmental appropriateness and child-centered learning. When approached about incorporating filmmaking into their classrooms, the teachers were enthusiastic but critical about how popular media production would fit into their program. The children's filmmaking experiences were different in each classroom, and the teachers' diverse approaches show the range of possibilities for preschool literacy play curricula.

Guided Engagements: Teacher Mediation in a Sea of Fluid Meanings

Karen and Sara provided filmmaking experiences throughout the school year in a variety of ways, both allowing children to film independently and guiding students through more elaborate film productions. *The Pirate Movie*, which opened the chapter, is one such example. It is easy to get caught up in the movie itself, a digital snapshot of children working together to present a story, but to truly appreciate the movie, we must turn our attention to the weeks-long process of creation.

Sara and Karen are astute kidwatchers, carefully watching the children in their charge. We call this "playwatching" to identify a focused form of kidwatching that notes the play themes children engage in as well as the ways they use materials in their pretense. Following repeated readings of *How I Became a Pirate* (Long, 2003), teachers noticed that pirate play surfaced in the children's free time, as swashbuckling children could be seen plundering and sailing the seven seas throughout the play space. Over the next few weeks, Karen, Sara, and the children engaged in a variety of literacy practices and story planning activities for *The Pirate Movie*—from making cast lists to designing costumes to singing a jaunty song titled "We Are the Pirates," which one child improvised to the tune of "Frosty the Snowman." With the children, Sara and Karen drafted a pirate play through multiple shared writing experiences in which teachers wrote the characters and their actions on an anchor chart, alternately teasing out or reining in plot actions in the script as the children told and retold the story around the story easel.

In one meeting to plan characters and props, Sara mediated an unexpected clash between play worlds. When she invited a group of pirate players to join her at the story easel to work on the cast list for their movie, one of the boys countered, "We're *knights* right now, not pirates." The children's passion and drive for the original pirate theme had, with the characteristic whimsicality of play, shifted to a different theme. The group of boys no longer embodied the pirates they had been so intent upon playing earlier. Sara, noticing this shift and wanting to move the project forward, adapted quickly, asking the students, "Well, can knights write a pirate play?" The knights agreed that indeed they could and clustered around her at the easel.

Shared writing of the list was also a fluid blend of play and literacy in a flexible space. That is, the children dressed in full knight regalia spent a few minutes making the list for *The Pirate Movie* with a teacher at the story easel, then moved back into their sword play and kingdom-defending in the dramatic play area, and then, having slain a villainous dragon or two, looped back to continue planning. Students with interests in particular characters or props made sure to stay near the teacher during planning.

During play, Sara acted as a co-player, noting the changes in pretense that children initiated while negotiating the story into directions that extended and supplemented previous play. Rather than a linear progression, the process of producing film was enmeshed within the ever-changing play of children within this preschool space. As a lead player, Sara sought opportunities to draw upon and validate the children's play through instructional moments that anchored the larger elements of the film, allowing children to move into and out of the production process as their play dictated. In the final recording, Sara mediated from within the story as a co-player:

The preschool pirates have climbed back aboard their pirate ship and begin counting down: "Five, four, three, two, one! Blastoff!" Hearing their cue, a quartet of girls sitting on the floor below the classroom loft begin slapping the tops of their legs with their hands while making a loud shushing sound, creating the audio backdrop for the intergalactic (another improvisation) pirate ship to take off.

"Captain, when are we there?" Sara, playing a member of the crew, calls out to the preschool pirates. Taylor, the captain, pauses and replies, "In seven, six, five...six minutes!"

"Six minutes?!" Karen calls from the audience.

"Now, we're going to ask the sea monster to get the treasure for us," Sara suggests. There is a flurry of action in the loft as the sea monster descends to the carpet, which has been imagined into an underwater scene.

The sea monster swims beneath the loft, retrieving building blocks wrapped in gold paper. He hands the gold to the pirates in the ship above, although their reception is lackluster. These pirates are not impressed with this gold. Noting this, Sara says, "We are so happy to have treasure, thank you, sea monster. Sea monsters are bringing us treasure."

Taylor, following this cue, exclaims, "Thank you, sea monster!" The other pirates do not mirror Taylor's appreciation and Sara continues: "Pirates, are you happy that you have treasure? Yay! Let me hear you!" The children now begin cheering as the sea monster climbs back aboard the ship and they prepare to blast off for treasure on another planet.

The teachers' emphasis during the writing of the story was to maintain its playful nature, which included children's improvisations to the story as the pirates morphed from generic archetypes to intergalactic plunderers. As mediators and meaning-holders for the filmmaking process, Sara and Karen were constantly working to make sense with their students over the course of this large film production and in other short-term projects, such as video commercials for a pretend café that the children created during a nutrition theme. This was not, however, the only way that teachers approached filmmaking in the preschool space.

Meaning Mediators: Supports for Media Production

To highlight instances of mediation that show how teachers helped individual children engage materials and peer cultures, we follow several children to provide a sense of their racial diversity and their developing language, literacies, and social relationships. Trevor, Laura, and Sam are white; Tommy is African American, Aliyah is biracial, and Hong Hong and Chih Wen are Asian American and English Language Learners. The children represent the variety of lived histories, technological capabilities, and social orientations within the peer cultures in these classrooms.

Trevor fits the profile of typically advantaged technology users. His media interests were supported at home, and he drew readily upon his knowledge of television programs for play, drawings, and stories at preschool.

Laura showed little interest in using classroom technology. She enjoyed pretend play, socializing with peers, talking with adults, and meeting new people; she eagerly introduced herself to the researchers and asked lots of questions about why we were recording classroom play.

Sam relied on pointing and other nonverbal actions, as well as short sentences, to communicate. He often experienced conflicts with other children during play. Cooperating and sharing materials with other children were challenging, in part, because he was more likely to take objects without asking rather than negotiate or share ideas verbally.

Tommy, one of the younger children in the class, played with a variety of groups but spent most of his time on the margins, watching and edging his way into existing play. When he came late to play already in progress, he was often delegated the "leftover" play roles at the dollhouse or building area.

Hong Hong and Chih Wen were avid fans of popular media and good friends. During choice time, the two boys frequently played together at the block center, building elaborate Transformers characters for battle and action. These creations—the most coveted materials in the block center—became status-enhancing mechanisms for the boys to interact with their peers.

Aliyah played frequently with a group of girls who engaged in princess play. Negotiations over who could play which princess became a key way that players positioned other group members, producing frequent conflicts between Aliyah and the blonde leader of the princess fans. In this way, highly popular media toys could be divisive and exclusionary, though Aliyah was able to leverage her technological abilities to gain access to this social space, something we will address later in this chapter.

Mediation as Just-in-Time and Just-Enough Teaching. Just down the hall from Sara and Karen's classroom, teachers Dawn and Michiru are also thoughtfully engaged in regular playwatching to negotiate literacy play curriculum with 20 3- to 5-year-old children. One early fall day, after 2 weeks working with video cameras, Dawn came to the teacher study group filled with excitement about a film she created with one of her preschoolers. During drawing time, Trevor had drawn the PBS Kids logo. Dawn noted, "He did that all by himself and that's what then prompted us to keep going [to follow his interest]. Trevor said, 'This is what I wanted to do.' " Recognizing his media knowledge as a literacy resource, Dawn helped Trevor create a *Wow! Wow! Wubbzy!* (nickjr.com) movie by scribing for him (i.e., writing his dictated script) as he drew the background setting on a long scroll of paper and also drew and cut out the characters. Figure 3.1 provides screenshots of Trevor's setting and characters, a transcript of Dawn's narration, and video description of the short film. (Moments when Dawn and Trevor's speech overlap are denoted by brackets.)

Figure 3.1. Wow! Wow! Wubbzy! Animated Film

Screen Capture of Storyboard	*Transcript*	*Video Description*
	Dawn: Wow Wow Wubbzy Treasure Hunt. Wow Wow Wubbzy... Wow Wow Wubbzy tells Widget and Walden ... What does he tell them?	A close-up of the scene.
	Trevor: There's no pirates in Wuzzleworld.	Each of the cut-out characters is added to the scene as they are introduced.
	Dawn: And then they goed on a trail. And then Wubbzy needed a parrot. And then Widget and Walden and Wubbzy saw some rocks. But they weren't rocks, they were...	Trevor moves the cut-out characters as though they were moving across the scene. Camera stops and focuses on what appears to be a pile of rocks.
	Trevor: [Snapping turtles.]	The child places a cut-out of a snapping turtle onto the paper.

(continued)

Figure 3.1. *(continued)*

	Screen Capture of Storyboard	Transcript	Video Description
5		Dawn: [Snapping turtle.] And Widget and Walden thought they didn't have any crackers but Wubbzy said…	Camera pans back to the trio of cut-out characters.
6		Trevor: "Oh, yes, we do have crackers!"	Trevor holds the cut-out of Wubbzy up to the camera, off of the paper. Wubbzy is placed back onto the paper once the line is delivered.
7	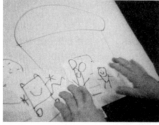	Dawn: And Wubbzy threw the crackers at the snapping turtles and the snapping turtles ate them. Trevor: The snapping *turtle*.	The camera moves from the trio to the turtle. Trevor then places crackers onto the cut-out of the turtle.
8		Dawn: The snapping turtle ate them. Then Widget and Walden and Wubbzy goed away from the snapping turtle before they stopped snacking. And that's the end.	The characters move to the end of the paper.

While the story is simple and, to an extent, a revoicing of the *Wow! Wow! Wubbzy!* episode "The Pirate Treasure," the methods of planning the movie were anything but simple. First, Trevor drew on a continuous piece of paper to represent the setting. The paper served as a storyboard as well as scenery, allowing Wubbzy and friends to progress through the movie; in essence, the characters themselves advanced along the paper as the story advanced. The characters, although made of paper and drawn in marker, resembled their Nick Jr. counterparts in terms of rounded edges and distinguishable shapes. Trevor moved the characters across the backdrop, animating them against the story's scenery. Wubbzy only left the paper backdrop when Trevor picked him up and moved him closer to the camera lens, an action-oriented and low-tech method of zooming in. Additional characters and props, such as a turtle and crackers to feed it, appeared as needed.

Dawn, acting as both teacher and film producer, narrated the story as Trevor animated the characters. Trevor voiced Wubbzy when Dawn invited him into the shared reading by pausing expectantly. She carefully narrated the story just as Trevor had dictated it, maintaining his authorship and honoring Trevor's developing grammar as she read "Wubbzy goed on a trail." She maintained the meaning of the story, taking responsibility for narration while Trevor moved the characters to play the story action. His action text was a sophisticated exploration that manually adjusted the composition of the shot image, manipulated the proximity of characters, and moved characters across the space of the backdrop. He appropriated the traditional materials of a preschool classroom—markers, paper, scissors—to create a movie that is both a revoicing of familiar popular media as well as a playful literacy event.

Trevor's film, when placed in conversation with *The Pirate Movie*, highlights the range of possibilities inherent in filmmaking in the preschool classroom. While *The Pirate Movie* was a large-scale production requiring a host of costumes and props, Trevor's film effectively used a restricted set of materials: paper and markers. The following vignettes show how mediation through filmmaking expanded the ways the preschoolers could play and participate.

Policy and Classroom Materials as Mediators. Michiru and Dawn worried at first, as many early childhood educators do, about the effects of bringing popular media toys into their classroom. They worried about the violent and sexist themes that popular media characters often carry, and about parent responses to these themes. When reflecting on the families their preschool served, Dawn noted, "We have a large camp for commercial-free childhood. And so I'm wondering how we [honor that concern]." Michiru agreed that parents who intentionally limited their child's television and Internet exposure would likely be wary of classroom projects that involved popular media. Sharing children's films with parents through online networks was not possible due to privacy and security concerns; preschool policy prohibited uploading child-made videos to the Internet, precluding a private YouTube channel for families.

The intersection of popular media and the early childhood classroom is contentious, in part because some popular media content, such as SpongeBob SquarePants, celebrates that which "adults consider to be rude, uncouth or gross" (Grace & Tobin, 1998, p. 43). Furthermore, children's interests in film may bring up politically sensitive topics that require responsive teaching. Inviting popular media—and the understandings about the world it promotes—into the classroom can amplify or shift power relations within the classroom: responsive teachers must use their professional judgment to consider the educational cost-benefit of particular media. Not all popular media should be brought into the classroom; conversely, not all popular media should be summarily excluded.

Beyond philosophical questions and parental concerns about childhood media exposure, there were practical issues of using technology in early childhood classroom settings. All four preschool teachers discussed ways to manage turn-taking among the children. Dawn pointed out that "there's going to be one [available video camera] in a classroom of twenty," resulting in children competing for 'My turn, my turn!' " Teachers also shared concerns about camera durability when handled by children. They wondered, laughing (but only half-joking), "Is it *throwing-proof?* Is it *stepped-on-proof?* Is it *water-table-proof?*" Ultimately they deferred to the decidedly child-led mission of their preschool and put cameras into the hands of children.

The teachers realized that popular media had already seeped into school— brought in by the children themselves—on backpacks and t-shirts, in conversations, and during play. This made media an important part of building an authentic home-school bridge. They viewed potential camera management challenges as opportunities to co-construct classroom expectations with their students. During one brainstorming session, Karen reflected,

> I think that's part of the lesson though, too…teaching the responsibility that goes with [camera use]. It gives us opportunities to come up with those rules: okay, we have this *one* [camera], you know, how do we use it? So it gives [the children] the opportunity to set the guidelines and boundaries as well.

Taking their cues from children's interests and experiences (and after much thought about logistics, equity, and child-centered pedagogy), Michiru and Dawn introduced a moviemaking center with one Flip video camera and a tub of *Toy Story 3* and *Dora the Explorer* action figures. The teachers chose these materials because they believed that many of the preschoolers would have viewed Toy Story and Dora programs outside of school. And in fact, when the center opened, several children piped up, "I have that show at home," hinting at the potential of the toys to provide literacy resources with rich characters, dialogue, and plots.

Like the teachers, our research team couldn't wait to see what children would come up with when cameras combined with toys during free play. We expected that children would need additional cameras and adult support to operate equipment, so after the media production center opened, our research team brought in one additional Flip video camera (for two cameras total) twice a week. What we didn't expect were the different ways the preschoolers would *own* the production process themselves, and that they would teach *us*.

All the adults involved in the project—six teachers in the three classrooms and all eleven members of our research team—held shared assumptions about what might happen when media play was integrated into early childhood classrooms. We assumed that very young children would eventually be capable of posing critical questions and making movies with their favorite popular media toys, but that it would take time to work up to this. We believed we would need to balance teacher mediation with child-led exploration, providing just-enough guidance on how to use the cameras while listening closely for children's media interests to help begin conversations. We knew that once cameras were introduced, filmmaking wouldn't happen automatically. Rather, we believed that children would need time to "play the play out" in the same way they need time to explore new math manipulatives or art supplies before being invited to do more focused tasks with those materials. But, eventually, we hoped that children would work up to storying in little individual or collaborative films that also played with typical popular media storylines and that those storylines could then be discussed and eventually critiqued.

However, over the course of the spring, we all adjusted our pacing and expectations in response to children's needs and interests. We found that when we let go of the expectation that these young children should produce movies with complete stories and a fixed, stable meaning, and instead privileged children's explorations with the materials, the outcomes were much richer and more complex.

Rules, Helpful Adults, and Peer Teachers as Mediators. On the first day the moviemaking center opened during free choice time, the preschoolers were already spread across the room busily playing at the sand table, water table, dramatic play area, dollhouse table, big blocks, and puzzles scattered on the floor. Dawn and a member of the research team, Rafi, put 12 Toy Story and Dora action figures in a tub at the center, set out two video cameras, and explained the rules to the interested preschoolers who wandered over: "These toys need to stay at the table, but if you want, you can bring props, blocks, dollhouses, or other toys to play *with* them from other areas of the room." Later, a second rule was added as a direct result of Michiru's "just-in-time" mediation. Michiru intervened in the following way in response to a child using the camera as a building block:

Michiru watches children's camera play as Sam makes the Diego doll teeter on top of his camera: "Humpty Dumpty sat on the wall, Humpty Dumpty had a great faaallll!" Sam hits the camera (play fighting), and Rafi asks him to be careful. Sam begins stacking the camera with other objects to make a tower. Michiru intervenes, talking about the difference between toys and cameras: "Cameras are not toys; they are tools for filming only." Michiru helps Sam get some blocks that he can use if he wants to build and Sam begins to play "King Kong" and "Donkey Kong," with the gorilla toy climbing up the blocks rather than up the camera.

Soon several interested children approached the table and picked up the cameras and toys to take a closer look. Teachers and researchers generally acted as mediators by watchful waiting— to explain, to spark children's interest, or to be helpful whenever the need arose:

Laura comes over and picks up a Dora the Explorer action figure, and Dawn asks,
"Who is that?"

"That's Dora," says Laura.

Rafi suggests, "This is the moviemaking table so you could make a movie with Diego and Dora and …"

Laura shakes her head "no," so Dawn asks her if she wants to make a movie but suggests that she can also just play with the toy figures.

A few minutes later, a group of boys approach the table. Dawn tells them there are special toys that need to stay at the table, but if the boys want to make a movie, they can. One boy inspects the Toy Story characters and announces, "I have that show at home."

As more children approach the table, Laura changes her mind, grasps the camera, and proclaims, "I turned it on!"

"You did!" exclaims Rafi. "Do you want me to show you guys how to make a movie?"

Dawn shows Laura how her finger is covering the camera screen while Rafi explains that she needs to record by pushing the red button. Laura then records Diego bopping around in a quick movie. Dawn tells Laura, "Now we can watch your movie. See, look. Let's press 'Play.' "

Laura and two more children crowd around the camera screen; smiles emerge as they rewatch the movie.

Sensing the children's interest, Dawn initiates another movie: "What do you think Diego could do in the next movie? Who's going to hold the camera?" A boy volunteers; this time, Laura will move the characters while someone records her.

In this way, helpful grown-ups facilitated children's exploration of technologies, mostly settling in nearby to assist as needed, and letting children go for it. By restricting themselves to the margins of children's play, the helpful grown-ups allowed space for the child's own agenda to emerge in relationship to both the toys and technology. Careful attention to the nature of children's play by the play-watching adult opens opportunities to extend and expand the play in meaningful ways, as is evident in Dawn's interactions with Trevor. Designing a filmmaking center, as described above, can be as simple as allocating space for popular media toys and a video recording device and a set of simple ground rules. As we saw in these classrooms, some children just played with the toys with little interest in the cameras, especially at first. They were more interested in getting their hands on Woody, Jessie, Buzz Lightyear, Bullseye, Dora, and Diego than in learning which buttons to push to record.

Aliyah and Sam were more interested than their classmates in the cameras. Their camerawork looked something like this:

As Sam films a short movie of Dora, Trevor, Hong Hong, and Chih Wen approach the filmmaking table and quickly and enthusiastically recognize some of the Toy Story characters. Rafi listens as Trevor explains that Evil Dr. Porkchop (the evil alter ego of the piggy bank) is the villain in Toy Story 3. Trevor announces quite expertly, "I have 1, 2, and 3 DVDs."

Hong Hong counters, "I don't. It's on my dad's phone. It's a Transformers movie on my dad's phone." Another child asks about the Dora the Explorer "Diego's Birthday" playset. Sam, who is still filming, thinks it's funny he can see his finger in the camera screen: "My finger is big!"

Aliyah plays out the story of Diego's birthday while pointing the camera toward her toy subjects and narrating her film. She asks Rafi, "How can you make pictures?" She successfully records her movie independently, and then plays the movie back immediately.

Aliyah then decides: "I want everybody to play them [use the toys], so I can press the buttons [concentrate on operating the camera]." Aliyah records Buzz Lightyear and other Toy Story characters as Tommy and another boy animate them for the camera. As soon as the movie is finished, the three children eagerly gather around the camera to review, or rewatch, their film.

Both Aliyah and Sam are particularly talented with the technology required of filmmaking, though each recognizes the multiple opportunities for participation available to students within the filmmaking process, most noticeably in Aliyah's request for her classmates to play with the toys so she may focus on filming. Eventually, as more and more children became interested in the technology, we saw them take up cameras in a variety of ways. With adult prompting and on-the-spot, just-in-time coaching, children filmed their neighbors' play or played out a "movie" in front of the camera, bobbing the action figures up and down in front of the lens and narrating their parts expressively as they might during playtime. This was the rarest use of the cameras, however, and usually accompanied by pretty heavy, individualized adult support. Coordinating camera operation with on-screen action was a lot for most children to juggle, even with adult assistance. Only Aliyah, who had extensive camera experience from home, was able to accomplish this easily. In fact, she was so skilled, she often took on the role of peer mediator:

Aliyah, Sam, and two other girls are at the filmmaking table. Aliyah asks Rafi, the helpful adult, how to record and then directs another child to "play with the people" while she records.

Aliyah begins recording the toy characters while her friend makes them speak: "It's Dora's birthday." Sam makes the birthday cake fly away, but Aliyah's camera turns off temporarily due to a low battery.

Another child tries to film this "'birthday play'" from the other side of the table, alternating between balancing the camera on its end and holding it carefully, peering intently at the viewing screen, without, however, actually pressing Record. Meanwhile, Aliyah continues to record different friends' play.

Aliyah gets help from Rafi to install new batteries, returning to the center to continue recording. She begins to assist an interested classmate in the functions of the camera, explaining the Record button and the viewing screen, pointing and demonstrating.

Using play as a conduit to filmmaking allows children to deliberately and thoughtfully take up roles that interest them. Trevor, for instance, attended to the material "stuff" of his Wubbzy film, focusing his energy on the creation of a background and characters while his teacher filmed the movie itself. Aliyah, conversely, invested her time and energy in the workings of the camera, more interested in the technical aspects of filmmaking. While Aliyah's singular interest in the camera established her as an expert within the classroom space, other children were interested in experimenting with the capabilities of the camera, though less intensely, reflecting a more typical experience in the moviemaking center.

Explorations at the Moviemaking Center

Experimenting with various functions was by far one of the most popular uses of cameras. When left to their own devices, preschool children spent the majority of their time flipping the USB ports in and out of the camera's side, turning the power on and off, and pressing the Record button rapidly and repeatedly to see the red numbers begin counting on the viewing screen. They also tested the scope of the camera lens by watching the world through the viewing screen and waving objects in front of it. They checked the sound recording abilities by speaking and yelling into the camera, making sound effects, using silly voices, and encouraging their friends to "say something" so it could be recorded and immediately played back.

Through immediate and frequent review of their work, children learned the capabilities of the cameras and discovered that their films could be transferred from one screen to another (e.g., from the small camera screen to a larger laptop screen). This realization was a first step in recognizing that media are produced by people operating cameras, an important building block in children's ability to engage in critical conversations about who makes popular media texts and why.

Besides tinkering with the functional capacity of the cameras, children also navigated the social aspects of filmmaking. This included negotiating:

- Who (or what) will be in the movie
- Who is the filmmaker, who holds the camera, and who controls the toys
- Who controls the reviewing process
- How turns are taken and how collaborative groups form

The end product of most preschoolers' media explorations, then, were a few short films of play dialogue and many, *many* nonsensical, blurry, bumpy, messy videos up to about 3 minutes long (and usually 1–7 seconds long). The majority of these "movies" were unplanned and often failed to contain a clear shot of an intended subject on the screen. There were lots of ceilings and fingers and floors, as well as extreme close-ups of the table at the moviemaking center. At other times, movies never even got *made* because figuring out how the Record button worked was too abstract for many preschool children to grasp, and though they thought they were "making a movie," they often found that no recording had happened at all. However, this had no bearing on the level of intention and engagement children brought to the process: the most organized and conventional directors might spend 10-20 minutes deliberately framing toys' actions and dialogue in the shot yet were unperturbed to find that the movie they thought they were making didn't exist because the Record button hadn't been pressed.

This put the developmental understanding of camera function that preschoolers brought to the project into sharp focus. The lack of a recorded film did not seem problematic for children; however, it was challenging for their adult mediators to figure out how best to explain or demonstrate the camera's perspective. Children often couldn't distinguish when the camera was on (screen capture mode) and when it was recording (record mode). They logically concluded that if they could see images on the screen, they must be recording. Also, they found it hard to believe when they were told that the moment they pressed the Record button, they had begun recording a movie that could be watched later. Somehow (but again, logically), they inferred that recording should look different on their screens. Since it was difficult for them to understand how the Record button worked, they usually just used it as something to push on/off, on/off, on/off rapidly. Trusting that the Record button could be pushed once and that the movie's playback abilities would start from that point was too abstract. Moreover, the fact that the same screens could be put into playback mode for reviewing films was an additional complexity that was difficult for preschoolers to understand. In the end, however, these were frustrations only for the "helpful" adults. The children had few expectations for the content of their films:

- They enjoyed seeing they had made a film.
- They delighted in hearing familiar voices replayed.
- They enjoyed recognizing familiar objects and people when those happened to be captured in the frame.

Most of all, children loved reviewing their movies. It didn't matter if videos were blurry "messes" of sound effects and laughter, or if they were only 3 seconds long. What mattered was the act of production. The preschoolers grasped the functionality of the cameras through play, and they could review the particular modes or elements of design that they had been testing moments before. Eventually, through peer mediation, playful experimentation, and reviewing, many children discovered that stable shots and longer films could be intentionally replicated.

Conceptualizing filmmaking as a developmental process helps shift focus from overemphasizing a final product to relishing exploration. These children are experimenting with the capabilities of the camera itself, just as they might experiment with the potentials of pencils, crayons, or paint when used in conjunction with paper. Through play, students have opportunities to begin developing an understanding of some fundamental concepts about media production, understandings that may not reveal themselves in final products, polished or not.

Revisiting Karen and Sara's preschool classroom provides a snapshot of students experimenting with media production embedded within play. Whereas Dawn and Michiru placed the camera at a moviemaking center, the moviemaking center in Karen and Sara's classroom moved across a variety of spaces and, for the most part, without adult mediation. Children often took the camera into other play centers, where the mini-explorations with technology resembled those in Dawn and Michiru's moviemaking center. For some children, the camera was simply a thing to be played with, no different than a block or baby doll. In these instances, children seemed less concerned with effectively recording their play than the novel view the camera gave them of their play. During a particularly complex play session with blocks in which the physical world of block play and the imagined vision of the camera were negotiated, two boys placed the camera in the middle of their play structure, a space that was so small neither of them would have been able to fit. With the camera, however, they were able to see another angle of their castle through the viewfinder, one happily exclaiming, "You see my castle!" For these children, the production of a final video product was of little consequence; rather, it was the understanding that the camera could allow them to see from a toy's perspective and imagine themselves as doll-sized players that mattered.

Multiplying Ways into Classroom Communities

Filmmaking allowed children to play to their strengths: Trevor employed his technology expertise behind the camera while Laura loved rewatching movies with an audience of friends and acting through popular media toys. However, teachers also wanted to bring children on the periphery of classroom culture into the center of the community. Through simple media production in these preschool classrooms, students on the social margins were afforded multiple ways "in" because of the multiple filmmaking roles available to the preschoolers. They could be players, producers, audience members, or a combination of these.

Consider, for example, Sam. In the moviemaking center, he found at least two ways in. First, though he could not operate the cameras conventionally, he tested audio-recording technology (pressing buttons rapidly, and shouting "Chicken nugget!" into the camera and then relistening). Camerawork carried status in the classroom space, both as a novel item in the classroom and as a signifier of control over production of the film. As such, an audience gathered to watch his attempts. Second, Sam drew upon his popular media expertise. That is, he knew the intended storylines for the Diego and Toy Story action figures, so he easily played those with peers while others recorded the action.

In the moviemaking center, as with the dollhouse and building centers, Tommy edged his way into play rather than taking the lead. Because the Toy Story action figures were familiar to him, however, he could access a popular play activity with more authority and participate on equal footing. He was also an avid audience member, laughing along with friends while reviewing and relistening to their recordings.

At the moviemaking center, Hong Hong and Chih Wen also easily entered the center of peer action by grabbing Buzz Lightyear and zooming him across the sky or by wordlessly battling opponent toys. They had family media experiences with Toy Story storylines, and used these as literacy resources in their play as a way to share their expertise and contribute to filmmaking with other children interested in either playing with the Toy Story figures or handling the cameras.

Aliyah had experience with technology and camera use from home that allowed her to take a leadership role in media production. This contrasted with her participation in the princess play group, where she faced exclusion or conflicts over desirable roles. She often assisted her peers in operating the cameras at the center and was herself an expert movie director/cameraperson. She seemed to enjoy her status as a highly sought-after technology expert, and came to the moviemaking center almost every day.

Through these examples, we can see evidence that children with a variety of abilities, strengths, and interests were afforded multiple opportunities to participate and succeed by playing different roles in media production. This is critical transformation at the level of classroom participation.

But we also wondered whether children were cognizant of their roles as budding media producers. Did they make connections between their participation in production and the people who made their favorite television shows and movies? At this point, probably not. Only fleeting conversations provided a glimpse of children's understanding, and the example that follows, in which Rafi approaches a group of children repeatedly reviewing a cluster of student-made videos, is a rare moment when a child put her thoughts into words.

RAFI: *So you guys are just watching videos … you don't want to make any?*

ALIYAH: *No. We love to watch TV!*

RAFI: *Is it like TV? How is it like TV?*

ALIYAH: *Because you get to see people acting up!*

[A discussion begins about how these videos are like/unlike TV.]

RAFI *[pointing to the film on the camera]: Who made this movie?*

ALIYAH: *I don't know.*

RAFI: *Was it the same people who made TV?*

ALIYAH: *[Our videos] are not like TV because they're just like "Raaarraar!" [indicating the cacophony emanating from the video] and it's like, a classroom!*

Aliyah concludes that the people on TV are not real but the people on the children's videos are real people in a real classroom. However, as we infer the extent to which students understood their roles as media producers, listening to their description was less revealing than watching them in action.

Conclusion

In this chapter, we documented some of the events occurring in preschool classrooms where children were engaged in filmmaking. It was fun and engaging for preschoolers to experiment with camera functionality, to review films (independently or with adult support), and to play with popular media toys in the classroom. Juggling all of those responsibilities to create a cohesive movie with steady shots and a sequential storyline became a burden that most preschool children didn't bother with when they were working independently. They seemed largely unconcerned with having a polished film product, delighting instead in the process and occasional collaboration with their peers. This independent exploration was perhaps the most intricate and complex form of media production the preschool children engaged in, as they morphed quickly from director, to cameraperson, to audience member, to critic, to actor, all within a few short minutes of play.

The fluidity we saw in children's explorations reflects the playful nature of their filmmaking. While children were engaging in the process of using cameras, popular media texts, and their own bodies to make movies, they adapted the processes to their own developmental abilities. This adaptability also flowed through their playful meaning-making in more structured, collaborative, and intentional guided production in *The Pirate Movie*. Large, collaborative projects such as this require much work by the teacher to maintain, negotiate, and adapt new manifestations of play as they arise in the classroom and influence the film. However, the experience of collaborating with teachers in the production process allowed the students to be mentored into the filmmaking process.

This chapter opened with a question of whether filmmaking is friendly to the negotiated, developmentally appropriate, and emergent curriculum in a child-centered preschool classroom. Drawing on their existing knowledge of popular culture texts, the children engaged in a variety of media production scenarios, from the small-scale production of the *Wow! Wow! Wubbzy!* movie to the large-scale production of *The Pirate Movie*. These preschool children were able to integrate filmmaking into their play within the supportive early childhood environments created by their teachers. Through thoughtful reflections and just-in-time mediation, teachers integrated filmmaking into playful preschool curricula in ways that were accessible to children, in tune with their interests, and embedded in their social worlds.

CHAPTER 4

The Literacy Playshop Framework

The mediation described in the previous chapters expands literacy learning and makes it relevant to modern childhoods by moving play and filmmaking to the center of the curriculum, with the aim of helping children produce and critically engage with popular transmedia. The Literacy Playshop framework draws upon sociocultural views of learning in which children learn the ways of "doing and being" (Gee, 2010, p. 16) that matter in their families, classrooms, and communities. According to Vygotsky (1978), children use literacies as cultural tools to access, understand, and make meanings as they learn to mediate the world.

Early childhood literacies include a wide range of *ways with words* (Heath, 1983), such as reading a book or sweeping across an iPad screen but also drawing a picture, playing with toys with friends, or watching a movie with family. These literacy practices are also social practices, which are valued ways of living and belonging in a particular culture. Literacies, then, include a variety of socially significant ways of managing tools—such as books, apps, crayons, video cameras, or toys—that produce meaningful texts, whether the fluid and temporary enactments in children's play or the fixed and durable print on a page.

Levels of Mediation

The concept of mediation includes teaching that provides a zone of proximal development, or the space between what a child can do alone and what that child can do with help (Vygotsky, 1978). The Literacy Playshop model offers three levels of mediation: child explorations, shared meaning mediators, and teacher guided engagements. Figure 4.1 illustrates the relationships between the levels: children's explorations at the center provide the creative power, mediated by tools that have been demonstrated by teachers in whole-group engagements. Recognizing that children are already experienced consumers, producers, and players, we begin with an inside-out orientation to teacher/student mediation that first recognizes the cultural expertise and media resources that are so evident in children's play.

Child Explorations. At the center of Literacy Playshop are messy but highly generative explorations that allow children to wander among stories, sounds, images, toys, and equipment—tapping a camera button on and off to hear it beep, playing with a word in a bit of remembered dialogue, rummaging through a tub picking up and discarding hand puppets. Like play, these wanderings are

Figure 4.1. Mediation Levels in Literacy Playshop

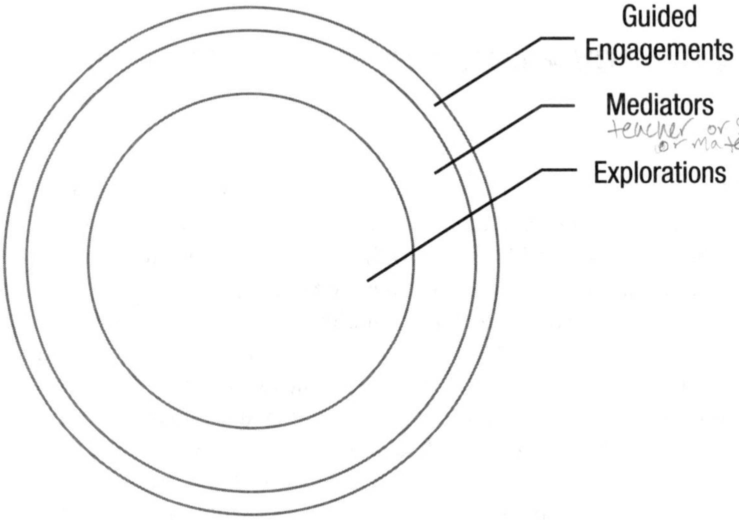

Guided
Engagements

Mediators
teacher or student
or material

Explorations

not orderly progressions but loopy transversals—zigzagging or spiraling across modes—that become key elements as children develop a co-constructed play narrative.

Explorations are a rich site for kidwatching during play, observing what children know and can do:

> It is the fuel for our desire to know more about the learning process as well as the continuous refinement of our craft as teachers. Kidwatching is not something apart from the curriculum but rather what holds it together and pushes it forward into new and often unexplored territory. (O'Keefe, 1997, p. 5)

Playwatching is the first step in teacher mediation. In the classrooms in which Literacy Playshop took place, teachers used playwatching to develop activities that picked up on children's play interests in popular media and to build on the richness of children's played texts.

Mediation that follows and responds to children's development requires regular time and sufficient space for children to play. The teachers in this study provided ample opportunities for children to play together and to explore materials. Open-ended explorations led to new discoveries, creating a natural progression as children moved into more expert storying and production. Exploratory play also opened up multiple pathways into literacy by providing more risk-free learning and a broader range of participation.

Shared Meaning Mediators. Over time, these explorations turn meaningful and produce mediators for literacy (Vygotsky, 1978); that is, the materials accrue shared meanings and uses so that cameras, puppets, or scripts not only come to stand for a character or a way of capturing actions or words but stabilize and represent a set of negotiations about who should say what or stand where. For example, a puppet becomes a mediator when it makes the player's hand motions meaningful and authorizes an expected way of interacting as a character in the play narrative as well as a role in the social group of players. Objects such as books, cameras, or toys come to stand for children's agreed-upon rules for retellings, play roles, turn-taking, or equipment-handling. These shared expectations allow children to proceed with less negotiation or clarification because all the players know what SpongeBob is supposed to say or do. Tools are mediators that preserve meanings in some way (via cameras, pencils, or iPads) or make meanings easier to communicate or understand (via storyboards, subtitles, or narration).

Mediators can be tools and materials, but teachers also mediate. Teachers mediate when they scribe or remember previously decided meanings and remind children about shared meanings, as Sara and Karen did in *The Pirate Movie*. Teachers mediate when they model or think aloud as they demonstrate new processes, as Doriet and Elizabeth did when introducing storyboards. Teachers mediate when they work with small groups to tease out multiple perspectives for a shared story or equitably resolve disputes about equipment use. Teachers mediate when they join in as co-players to support play frames in-character, as Sara did during pirate play. Teachers mediate by reflecting on their power in the classroom and questioning whether they are usurping children's authority to control the story or to play out issues of importance to children (Wohlwend, 2009).

Mediation straddles the space between teacher-guided engagements and child explorations. Teachers in all classrooms talked about the challenge of maintaining a cohesive story meaning amid the fluidity of children's play, reminding us of the metaphor "nailing Jell-O to a wall." But they also were very aware of the need to allow children to own the story and change directions as they wished. When mediation leans too far in either direction, it feels artificial and forced or chaotic and aimless. For example, the teachers critiqued their initial attempts to lead children in problematizing gendered texts (e.g., the boy-girl toy sort in the K/1 classroom discussed in Chapter 2). From the teachers' perspectives, their initial mediation felt too teacher-directed and imposed, and seemed to reinforce binary gender categories. They felt more successful in bridging home and school cultures, either by researching and incorporating children's favorite toys and known storylines or by inviting families in to share their expertise.

Teacher-Guided Engagements. At the outer level of the Literacy Playshop model, teachers use guided engagements to introduce and demonstrate ways of using and thinking about media, but sparingly, just-in-time and just-enough, informed by their kidwatching. Similar to shared reading or writing experiences in reading and writing workshops, guided engagements provide shared experiences that scaffold children into new literacies. Working with the whole class also allowed teachers to alleviate the intense investments of teacher time and attention that were needed to help individual children or small groups manage new forms of technology. By providing a shared filmmaking experience, children gained enough experience to work in small groups where peers could further support one another.

Demonstrations in guided engagements also sparked more explorations as new materials and practices were introduced. In this way, Literacy Playshop provides a recursive space for children to lead through exploration, for teachers to build on children's media expertise and developing literacy abilities, and for players and producers to tap into their own media knowledge.

Processes of Meaning-Making with Media

The child-centric orientation to Literacy Playshop reflects our experiences as early childhood educators rather than as filmmakers or media studies scholars. For example, instead of emulating a production cycle that follows a standard film industry sequence of preproduction, production, and postproduction, which characterizes media education, we situate our model in the fluid meanings and topsy-turvy relationships of young children's play worlds.

In Literacy Playshop, four processes contribute to children's meaning-making with media: play, storying, collaboration, and production. While the three levels of mediation move inside out and back again, the four processes are represented here as loosely defined domains, so there is no production sequence or curricular "cycle" but, rather, recursive connections that spread across domains in multiple and unruly directions. Each of the four processes contributes a critical, productive, and interdependent aspect of meaning-making that also links to a larger curricular field: drama, literature, diversity and community, and media and cinema arts (Figure 4.2).

Play allows children to work on a text as characters within an imaginary scenario and creates co-authored embodied meanings built moment to moment. Criticality emerges from a tension among players' multiple perspectives (Lewison, Flint, & Van Sluys, 2002) in the enactment of a coherent shared meaning. Finally, play provides a way of imagining otherwise to try out new ways of doing things (Medina & Wohlwend, in press).

Storying makes a text durable, similar to writing in print- and image-based meanings in literature. Storying draws children's attention to literary structures such as character, plot, setting, theme, and so on. While teacher-student conferences and child-made books are tried and true supports for writing workshop, Literacy Playshop highlights embodied shared meanings captured with film tools

Figure 4.2. Media Processes in Literacy Playshop

such as photos, scripts, and storyboards that record action and dialogue. The term *storying* is used rather than storytelling to encompass the multiple modes and conventions in verbal storytelling, visual storyboarding, and embodied drama.

Collaboration is the hallmark of participatory literacies such as play, so that the meanings and roles in multiplayer pretense, live-action dramas, and films are constantly subject to improvisation and renegotiation. Collaborative structures provide the means for seeing others' perspectives and shared decision-making that opens up negotiations.

Production refers to all aspects of camera work and film editing and includes supports such as user-friendly hand-held video cameras or digital tablets and film editing software like iMovie or Movie Maker.

Play and Shared Meanings. Play complements the daily demonstrations and scaffolded participation that teachers and parents provide, creating a child-governed space to sort through and explore cultural meanings of adult worlds.

Children's collaboration with competent members of the society help children decide what meanings are worth engaging in as well as how to engage in those meanings. Children's play, on the other hand, enables children to internalize the meanings that children consider on their own as worth engaging in. (Göncü, 1999, p. 11)

In their pretend play, children can replace an object's conventional meaning with a new meaning. For example, the meaning of a 1-yard square of red cloth in the dramatic play corner fluidly shifts from its conventional use as a kitchen tablecloth to a mother's wraparound skirt to a baby's blanket to a mermaid's hair within the space of several minutes. These shifts depend on a common history of accepted meanings for tablecloths, blankets, or costumes that produce the "multivoicedness of meaning" (Wertsch, 2001, p. 66), allowing alternate meanings to be accessed and inscribed in a given moment of activity. Because the meanings of our actions are dynamic, socially constructed and ongoing, they are always subject to changing interpretations.

The polysonic and fluid nature of play produces opportunities for individual agency and transformation through slippages and shifts of meaning that allow people to twist meanings of objects, and to also change the context (Sherzer, 2002). However, these imagined meanings also require the cooperation and acceptance of other players. In play, children must work together to sustain shared meanings—interpretations of events or texts that are discussed and collaboratively accepted—as they talk and enact scenes. In similar ways, children's media productions require negotiations among actors, directors, and camera persons to maintain a sensible and cohesive collectively produced text.

Storying in Multiple Modes. When children play a story, they represent meanings through speech, action, sound effects, movement, props, and the layout of the physical environment. When they transfer their play to paper in the form of storyboards or scripts, their rich play meanings are constricted by the need to represent live-action texts with pencil and paper. We found that children showed renewed interest in story when teachers let go of the need for children to put ideas in writing and to fix their play meanings in print. Storying is a multimodal orientation to meaning that affords multiple pathways to literacy by offering a choice of features to notice and a rich array of materials to explore.

Even when we read print, we read multimodally, responding to the texture of the page, the shape of the letters, the linearity of the print, the visual layout of the page, the sound of the language, and so on. However, print literacy can only convey textual information, while video and animation require design and coordination of modes of speech, image, sound effect, movement, camera angles, physical space, and so on (Kress, 1997, 2003). Children regained control of their stories when teachers expanded what counted as recording to include storyboards, set construction, and voice and sound effects or expanded what counted as production to include live action, block play, or *Wow! Wow! Wubbzy!* paper cutouts moving along paper scenery. In crafting their sets, characters, and videos, children were resourceful users of the space and materials as they considered three-dimensional aspects of their stories.

When Elizabeth and Doriet challenged the literacy 1.0 mind-set of individual authorship, they questioned the need to proceed through a sequence of continual revision of a single piece of writing. Instead, as children played stories, they revised prior meanings even when working on new stories and films. In preschool explorations, we saw children revise through play, so that stories were revisited but still made fresh daily. Even when playing with the same toys, children experimented with a new context, plot twist, or characters. The power in this shift from print to play representation is the way it repositions the child who seems stuck for ideas to a child who is frustrated by effectively representing action texts within the shackles and reductive conventions of a print paradigm.

Collaboration and Negotiated Participation. Given the multiple modes, slippery meanings, and plastic worlds of pretend play, playing a co-constructed and cohesive action text is a challenge. When two or more children collaborated in play, they often found that they needed to stop to clarify shared meanings, propose new roles or props, orchestrate the sequence of turns in enactments, clarify roles, or redirect play storylines. Early childhood classroom studies show that dramatic play and collaborative talk create a collective sphere of emerging and changing meanings and relationships shaped by children's negotiations (Dyson, 2003a; Martin & Dombey, 2002; Sawyer, 1997).

The need to clearly define meanings causes children to stop playing to negotiate their character roles and agree upon the meanings of their props before shifting back into pretense. Vygotsky (1978) theorized that this kind of symbolic play with meanings is a "particular form of speech...which leads directly to written language" (p. 111). We update this proposition to argue that pretend play with its negotiated and co-constructed texts links directly to participatory digital literacies that underlie social media. Collaboration captures an important shift in literacy practices: from viewing a media text as an outside audience member to interacting within the text with co-actors and co-producers or interacting with a media product and brand as a fan and a consumer.

Media Production with New Technologies. According to Bazalgette (2010),

> Children's early media experiences are an important part of their introduction to our culture: the shared ways of thinking and telling that bind us together...[these experiences also reveal] what the children value and what they are good at. (p. 7)

Children's expertise is rooted in an expanded orientation to meaning-making that includes conventions of time-based texts (film, television, video games, virtual worlds) of popular media, not just conventions of page-based texts (books, newspapers, web pages, posters) of schooling. In this view, the focus is not on the technology but on the literacies that interpret juxtaposition of subjects within a shot, transitions between shots, soundtracks and sound effects, and so on.

Modern childhoods are steeped in digital media; however, children most often engage in listening, viewing, reading, or playing with films, video games, or electronic toys that adults have designed *for* them. Typically young children are not encouraged to create their own original digital media (Nixon & Comber, 2005). Even in the classrooms in this study, it took time to get cameras in the hands of children. The teachers and the researchers shared assumptions about production that circulated through dominant models of performance and authorship. *The Pirate Movie* drew upon the model of a school pageant with its teacher-led rehearsal and final performance for parents, although it was an irrepressibly playful version of a pageant. Similarly, in the K-1 classroom, storyboarding and film production began with a writing workshop model of a simulated apprenticeship in book publishing. Both pageant and workshop models became confining for the teachers, causing them to reevaluate and expand these approaches oriented to a child's-eye view of production. From this perspective, teachers uncovered new understandings as children discovered that film was not merely a moving image on screen, but a medium with special affordances that allowed them to:

- Review the video after shooting the footage;
- Share the video with others;
- Transfer video to other screens (computer, iPad, and so on) and show it somewhere else; and
- Capture and recognize real places and actions of real people.

Children also learned the constraints of film:

- Cameras record only a fraction of what can be seen through the lens;
- Things recorded at a distance may not be visible on screen; and
- Cameras must be aimed and record buttons pushed in order to create video.

We approach media production with the same appreciation of inventive development that we apply to literacy learning. We expect invention and "playing at" filmmaking as children approximate the media forms that they know from everyday life.

Valuing Children's Developing Literacies and Teachers' Expertise

The children who have been discussed in the previous chapters were deeply engaged in making media and becoming producers. Over the year, the teachers believed that children gained a better appreciation of commercial texts as produced and that this awareness could represent an initial—and perhaps more developmentally appropriate—step toward a more critical view of popular media. We did not see children articulating critiques of their favorite media, but they were coming to their own sense of what it means to produce a meaningful text in collaboration with others as they negotiated peer culture relationships. As discussed in the previous chapters, we could see peer culture effects that expanded participation for all children. Literacy Playshop provided multiple entry points for children—as players, storytellers, set designers, prop-makers, directors, camera operators—in ways that encouraged the use of children's diverse literacy resources, interests, and expertise.

In an era when teacher expertise is repeatedly devalued through highly scripted curricula (Allington & Pearson, 2011), prescriptive legislation (Ravitch, 2010), and reformist films such as *Waiting for Superman* (Swalwell & Apple, 2011), it is important to reclaim teachers' professional judgment and knowledge. Just as teachers recognized and built on children's knowledge and experiences with technology and popular media, policymakers, administrators, and parents need to empower teachers to draw upon their professional judgment and kidwatching skills that make responsive teaching possible. Through Literacy Playshop, teachers were able to build on their teaching experiences and pedagogical knowledge of familiar instructional models, such as writing workshop and developmentally appropriate practice, as strong foundations for creating a new model. The teachers' inventions and innovations were grounded in beliefs about children as active and knowledgeable learners who can be trusted to explore productively, to collaborate, and to teach one another.

Conclusion

The Literacy Playshop model provides interconnected opportunities for exploration, paired with modeled demonstrations and just-in-time mediation that connects children to their playful literacies, popular media storying, collaborative teamwork, and new technologies. Figure 4.3 illustrates how varying levels of mediation support the four domains needed to create digital films. The classroom examples show the power of Literacy Playshops to expand the range of school literacies made available in early childhood classrooms. The sample curricular activities in the Literacy Playshop Components chapters that follow demonstrate how to set up and facilitate learning through teacher inquiry, guided engagements, meaning mediators, and explorations. We hope the examples and activities in this book will inspire and support teachers in developing Literacy Playshops that redefine and update literacy tools, classroom social structures, and meaning-making processes focused on collaboration, collective knowledge, play-based learning, and new media literacies.

Figure 4.3. Literacy Playshop

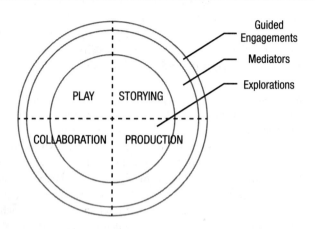

Literacy Playshop Components

The table below breaks down the Literacy Playshop Components:

Levels and Processes	Teacher Inquiry Activities	Guided Engagements	Mediators	Explorations
Play	Playwatching and Popular Media Audits	Playing Action Scripts with Puppets3	Puppets Costumes and Props Playsets and Dolls Play Videos and Photoboards*	Made Fresh Daily: Talking Hands Using Cameras as Toys Playing Filmmaker Animating with Paper, Scissors, and Tape SkypePlay*
Storying	Critically Reading Toys as Texts	Mapping Story in Film Shorts with Storyboards	Cast Lists, Sets, and Meaning Anchors Photo Puppets Picture Books as Mentor Texts Animated Stories and Character Cut-Outs Digital Puppets*	Respecting Storying as Exploratory Process: Sequencing Storyboards Making Scenery with Propped-Up Books Storying with Illustrations and Stills Commercial Media Screenshots*

(continued)

Levels and Processes	Teacher Inquiry Activities	Guided Engagements	Mediators	Explorations
Collaboration	Building Support for Play	Negotiating Meaning with Popular Media Toys	Time for Playing Together Teachers as Mediators and Co-Players Peer Negotiation Structures Peer Experts Class Heart Map and Audit Trail Wordle*	Exploring Ways to Collaborate: Cooperating with Cameras Re-watching Together on Mobile Screens Projecting from Tablets to TVs*
Production	Analyzing Film Meanings	Editing Film and Creating Sound Effects	Digital Cameras, Tablets, and Apps Director's Commentaries*	Bubbles of Filmmaking: Seeing Like a Camera Making Sound Effects and Funny Voices Pushing Buttons Wireless Microphones*

* Technology Try-It

The components in this part of the book cover the levels in the Literacy Playshop framework: Guided Engagements, Mediators, and Explorations. Component 1 addresses all three levels through overarching Teacher Inquiry, or professional development. Subsequently, Component 2 offers activities at the level of teachers-guided engagements, Component 3 addresses the middle level of mediators, and Component 4 describes children's explorations in the inner level.

Furthermore, each Component provides specific activities for each process: Play, Storying, Collaboration, and Production. At the beginning of each process section, a model of the Literacy Playshop framework appears in the upper corner, shaded to locate the corresponding level and process. For example, the first Teacher Inquiry Activity in Component 1 involves investigating and planning for all three levels of play so the full play quadrant of the model is shaded.

Teacher Inquiry Activities

Teacher inquiry activities are designed for teachers who want to form their own teacher-study group or to develop and implement Literacy Playshops. Teacher inquiry activities are provided for each process: play, storying, collaboration, and production. Each teacher inquiry activity includes a stated purpose, a description of the activity, the materials needed, and a "Technology Try-It"—an exploratory extension using digital tools.

Playwatching and Popular Media Audits

Playwatching, a specialized version of kidwatching, is systematic observation that provides teachers with the information needed to provide culturally responsive teaching and learning. But it is much more:

> It is valuing the contributions each child makes within the learning community that is our classroom. It is helping children realize who is an expert at what and who they can turn to when they need assistance. It is giving voice to students who might otherwise be silent. It is getting to know each child in as many different contexts as possible— to know each child as a person unique in all the world. (O'Keefe, 1997, p. 5)

Purpose: To discover students' media interests

Description: Begin playwatching by observing what children say, do, wear, and play and noting who plays with whom.

Audit children's popular media interests by making lists of transmedia and noting clues from the following sources:

- Students' clothing and accessories
- Students' school supplies: backpacks, lunch boxes, pencils, notebooks (including the occasional contraband toy from home)
- Students' play: themes pretended at recess and other free choice periods, including imaginary play
- Students' classroom talk: popular characters discussed with friends or teachers

Discover particular children's expertise so that you can build bridges to curricular activities and also to help them access their expertise to join play groups with ideas for character roles or storylines. (For an observational checklist for play, see Wohlwend, 2005.) Often children are experts on a wide variety of media characters that adults may not know. To find your media experts, ask sincere questions about children's transmedia items such as, "What does that character do? Is that from a TV show or a movie? What channel is it on?"

Make a list of popular media and lead characters that children know and love. Simply knowing what children are interested in will open up an entire realm of critical, emergent, play-based learning possibilities for you.

Spend time learning more about some of these characters by doing Internet research and watching television shows and movies. If you form a teacher study group, you can examine multiple media storylines for literacy potential as you pool your knowledge about media resources.

Suggested Readings for Teacher Study Groups

Owocki, G., & Goodman, Y. M. (2002). *Kidwatching: Documenting children's literacy development.* Portsmouth, NH: Heinemann.

Wohlwend, K. E. (2005). Chasing friendship: Acceptance, rejection, and recess play. *Childhood Education, 81*(2), 77–82.

Selected Children's Media Resources

Television Shows

- PBS: http://www.pbs.org/parents/tvprograms/pbskids/
  Sesame Street, Curious George, Sid the Science Kid, Super Why!, Dinosaur Train, Caillou, The Wiggles
- Nickelodeon: http://www.nick.com/shows/
  SpongeBob SquarePants, Penguins of Madagascar, Blue's Clues, Power Rangers, Neopets
- Nick Jr.: http://www.pbs.org/parents/tvprograms/pbskids/
  The Backyardigans, Bubble Guppies, Dora the Explorer, Team Umizoomi, Ni Hao, Kai-lan, Wow! Wow! Wubbzy!, Peppa Pig
- Disney Junior: http://disney.go.com/disneyjunior/
  Doc McStuffins, Jake and the Neverland Pirates, Octonauts, Handy Manny, Special Agent Oso, Disney Princess, Toy Story, Little Einsteins
- The Hub: http://www.hubworld.com/
  Care Bears, Transformers, My Little Pony, Strawberry Shortcake, Pound Puppies
- Cartoon Network: http://www.cartoonnetwork.com/tv_shows/index.html
  Adventure Time, Power Puff Girls, Star Wars: The Clone Wars, Lego Ninjago: Masters of Spinjitzu, *Batman, Pokémon*

Movie Franchises

Disney Princess, Toy Story, Spider-Man, Star Wars, Cars, Shrek, Batman, Pirates of the Caribbean, Ice Age, Superman, Spy Kids, Transformers, Barbie

Video Game and Virtual World Franchises

- Super Mario Brothers: http://mario.nintendo.com/
- Angry Birds touchscreen mobile game apps
- Club Penguin: http://www.clubpenguin.com/
- Webkinz: http://www.webkinz.com/

Play Audit Questions

Which media toys do children bring to school?

Which media franchises or characters decorate children's clothing, backpacks, or school supplies?

Which popular media characters and themes are evident in:

pretend play in classroom play centers?

trading, sharing, or play on the playground?

children's drawings or storytelling?

movies, video games, books, or songs children know and talk about?

Who plays which popular media? How do children's play groups intersect with particular media themes?

How do children negotiate access to popular media toys or activities?

Technology Try-It: Wikipedia and YouTube

Sometimes browsing a television show or video game through its Wikipedia page is a good way to get an overview of a vast popular media franchise, including its many versions and spinoffs. On YouTube, you can find "Let's Play" videos in which players demonstrate video games and narrate as they play. To find these playthroughs, type in a video game title with the letters LP in the search bar.

Critically Reading Toys as Texts

In her 2004 book, Vivian Vasquez describes how she and her preschool students used critical literacies to read Happy Meal toys as texts, with the goal of understanding how McDonald's capitalizes upon children's love of toys and popular culture to market hamburgers. The following excerpt illustrates young children's ability to understand commercial strategies (Vasquez, 2004, p. 127):

> *Curtis:* They always change the toys.
> *Teacher:* Why do you think they do that?
> *Ali:* Well, maybe it's because they know we like toys.
> *Teacher:* Do you mean children like toys or adults or both?
> *Ali:* I think both but mostly kids. That's why there's toys in Happy Meals.
> *Tiffany:* Yah, that's why.
> *Andrew:* Well, if they didn't change the toys I wouldn't go.
> *Michael:* Me either.
> *Andrew:* Actually that tells me McDonald's knows how we think! But now, now, we know how they think. Aha!

The fast food industry uses children's media passions to sell hamburgers and fries, spending nearly $294 million on promotions in one year (Marr, 2008). By contrast, educators often know little about what makes popular media so appealing to children. How can you use these toys to engage children's interests but also to help them see the messages embedded in these toys?

Purpose: To raise critical awareness of the identity texts prepackaged in popular media toys

Description: Look closely at a popular transmedia toy, such as the promotional toys included in children's fast food meals. The first challenge is to get it out of the plastic packaging, assemble it if necessary, and figure out what it does.

Share what you have discovered about the toy and demonstrate its use with your teacher study group. If you don't recognize the character or the popular media franchise it represents, ask your peers to see if anyone does.

After everyone shares, work with a partner or in a small group to explore the toys, using the following questions (Wohlwend & Norton-Meier, 2007) as a guide:

Questions to Interrogate a Happy Meal Toy

1. What is the toy's expected use? (the authorized use that its producer intends)
2. What else could you do with it? (unauthorized uses that consumers imagine)
3. What sort of play does the toy encourage?
4. What kind of space do children need to play with it?
5. What would children learn about being a boy or a girl while playing with this toy?
6. What sensory qualities in the materials would make children want to play with it?
7. What do children need to know in order to play with it?
8. Are there other toys or media that children would need to have?
9. What would children (or parents) need to buy to complete the collection?
10. What media would children (or parents) need to buy, and how many times would they need to view, play, or listen to the media to know the "official" storylines?
11. How strong is the toy and how long will it last?
12. Does it come with instructions or safety information?
13. What's the "pester power" potential of this toy (the child's desire for a toy that will drive a parent to buy a fast food meal)?
14. What's the cost? Is it free? What automatically comes with it that you wouldn't otherwise want?
15. What do you know about the popular media or franchise related to this toy?

Consider what you've learned about popular media toys and reflect: What opportunities for critical study could you create by allowing these toys and their stories into your classroom?

Materials: Fast food toys with original packaging, one per participant

Suggested Readings for Teacher Study Groups

Vasquez, V. M. (2004). *Negotiating critical literacies with young children.* Mahwah, NJ: Erlbaum.

Vasquez, V. M., & Felderman, C. B. (2012). *Technology and critical literacy in early childhood.* New York: Routledge.

Wohlwend, K. E., & Hubbard, P. (2011). Reclaiming play: Reading toys as popular media texts. In R. J. Meyer & K. F. Whitmore (Eds.), *Reclaiming reading: Teachers, students, and researchers regaining spaces for thinking and action* (pp. 241–255). Mahwah, NJ: Erlbaum.

Technology Try-It: Commercial Toy Websites

Using the questions listed above, analyze corporate websites to uncover the messages conveyed in marketing popular toys to children.

Building Support for Play

Pam Hubbard (Wohlwend & Hubbard, 2011) found that a proactive approach worked well to convince administrators of the value of play in her kindergarten. When a new assistant principal walked by two boys playing with Transformers, he did a double-take but said nothing and walked on. Wondering what he thought, Pam waited for a "teachable moment." It came a few days later when two boys were ready to perform their play about Transformers. Pam invited the assistant principal, and the boys explained how the project evolved from playing and writing about the toys.

Purpose: To build support for play-based learning in the classroom, especially with popular media toys

Description: Teachers found multiple strategies useful in meeting the dominant challenges to implementing filmmaking: access, accountability, and appropriateness of popular media. As a starting point, consider the following strategies.

Form Teacher Study Groups. Find other teachers who are interested in expanding their literacy curriculum and meet *regularly*. Getting together allows you to share similar issues that pop up across classrooms, discuss teaching responses, and question and affirm one another's teaching—all crucial for working against isolation when trying a new approach.

    The *study* in teacher study groups matters. Understanding current research is key to effectively advocating for play in your classroom. Teacher study groups can read and discuss recent research on media and new literacies, analyze media clips and popular toy designs, coach one another in filmmaking production skills, and develop curriculum together.

Bring Your Own Toys. Invite children to bring their favorite (popular media or other) toys into the classroom so they can play and film stories. (It is important to note that the toys are not for a "show-and-tell" sharing session but literacy tools; that is, props and characters for the play and films that children produce.) The bring-your-own-toy strategy inherently honors families' views by limiting toys to the kinds of popular media they allow their children to have. You may also wish to provide additional toy sets for children who do not have or bring their own toys. We noticed that classroom sets of media toys such as the Dora and Diego or Toy Story playsets were highly popular for the first few days but soon lost their novelty and became more useful for representing characters and story action.

Team with Parents and Administrators. Communicate proactively with parents and administrators by previewing upcoming filmmaking activities in classroom blogs and newsletters. Sharing the educational rationale behind these activities can demonstrate how media toys bridge children's areas of literary expertise and support specific school literacy goals and standards.

Materials: School policy documents on media; classroom blogs and newsletters

Suggested Readings for Teacher Study Groups

Fernie, D., Madrid, S., & Kantor, R. (Eds.). (2011). *Educating toddlers to teachers: Learning to see and influence the school and peer cultures of classrooms.* Cresskill, NJ: Hampton Press.

Wohlwend, K. E. (2010). A is for avatar: Young children in literacy 2.0 worlds and literacy 1.0 schools. *Language Arts, 88*(2), 144–152.

Technology Try-It: Social Media and Class Blogs

Social media enables global collaboration with early childhood educators who help one another strategize and advocate for play and digital literacies. The exemplary Twitter community #kinderchat, founded in 2010 by kindergarten teachers Heidi Echternacht and Amy Murray, is both a supportive chat and a professional learning network.

Document and share digital photos or clips of filmmaking in action on class blogs or websites, or family Facebook groups, which are private groups for students' families only. Be sure that digital sharing aligns with your school's policies on social media and parental permissions. Timely posts allow parents and children to talk about the school day's events and bring parents into the life of the classroom in ways that help them appreciate children's playful engagement and learning. Matt Gomez, another #kinderchat leader, maintains a class blog that is packed with early childhood technology teaching ideas at http://mattbgomez.com/

Analyzing Film Meanings

Meanings in films are conveyed through the ways that shots are arranged in sequences that make up scenes, similar to the scale relationships between words, sentences, and paragraphs. For example, a first shot in a scene might begin with a long shot that shows a landscape or a view of a room that explicitly and calmly establishes the context. In contrast, a scene that begins in the middle of the action with a medium shot of a character's face and torso can be purposefully unsettling and suspenseful, causing viewers to wonder what's going on and what's going to happen next.

Storyboards are drawings of shots in sequence. Storyboarding with young children should focus on quick sketches that quickly capture characters, action, and the flow of the story, rather than neatness or completeness. Storyboards are most effective when children find them useful as anchors for a text but can also improvise on the storyboard's planned action.

Purpose: To see how film elements (shot types, sequence, and scene) fit together meaningfully in short commercials or film trailers for popular media

Description: Consult media literacy resources, such as the books listed below or websites such as www.mediacollege.com/video/shots, to understand film shots and their importance.

With other interested teachers, watch a commercial or film trailer to see how meanings are shaped by the kinds of shots used and the ways those shots fit together. Discuss the various meanings that viewers take away. For example, see McDonald's short commercials for Happy Meal toys: http://www.happymeal.com/en_US/index.html?#Video_Page.

Watch the film several times, pausing the video to identify a few shots, and to notice how each shot relates to other shots in the sequence and how this interaction contributes to the overall effect.

Record a short sequence of shots on a storyboard.

Rewatch the video and discuss how the choice of shots and sequencing promotes particular meanings and emotional responses.

Materials: Laptops or iPads for partner or small-group viewing; storyboard templates with six frames or papers folded lengthwise in half and then crosswise into thirds to create six panels

Suggested Reading for Teacher Study Groups

Black, K. (1989). *Kid vid: Fun-damentals of video instruction.* Brookline, MA: Zephyr Press.

Scheibe, C., & Rogow, F. (2012). The teacher's guide to media literacy: Critical thinking in a multimedia world. Thousand Oaks, CA: Corwin.

Technology Try-It: Animation Apps

Toontastic is an iPad app that allows children to animate short videos by recording their voices while moving characters across sets, with immediate playback. Scenes are created separately and combined into a film in the final step. Children can upload their movies or watch other child-made videos on Toontube (http://toontube.launchpadtoys.com/). Consider using parental controls such as Guided Access under iPad settings to limit children's use to a specific app.

Guided Engagements

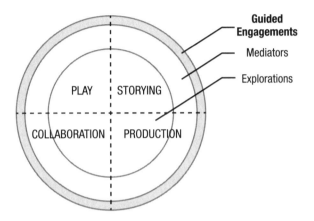

Guided engagements are activities planned and led by teachers but with significant contributions by children. As in the previous section, an activity is provided for each process; each includes a stated purpose, a description of the activity, the materials needed, and a Technology Try-It.

Playing Action Scripts with Puppets

Remember the writing adage: show, don't tell? The goal here is to let character actions, body language, and eye contact tell the story. Puppets are great tools for helping children understand how actions communicate. Ideally, narration should be used sparingly (e.g., for explaining characters' motivation or revealing their hidden thoughts. Think of the character motivation and thoughts shared by the narrators of *Grey's Anatomy* and *Desperate Housewives*).

To play action meanings through puppetry, children need good-quality hand puppets with moving mouths and arms. The stick or felt hand puppets so popular in early childhood classrooms don't allow action to carry much meaning; child-drawn paper figures bouncing across a puppet stage often make little sense to other players or audiences.

In addition, puppets draw out and tap into children's play dialogue, which often uses bits of realistic adult conversation or familiar dialogue from media scripts and songs. The focus here is not on making children *write* scripts but on finding ways to inspire and connect *action* and *talk* through puppetry and then capture snippets of their rich play narratives in nonreductive ways.

Purpose: To focus on how characters move and act to help tell the story

Description: With a small group, help children manipulate puppets to carry the story. Using a hand puppet and puppetry demonstrations (see the YouTube examples in the "Materials" section), show children techniques to convey meanings through actions that simulate eye contact, body language, and emotion.

Select a portion of a children's book and use it with a small group as inspiration to co-construct an action script for a puppet show. Encourage children to improvise puppet movements to act out the book as a puppet show.

Use your own puppet to demonstrate how puppets can move to appear to interact with other characters. Try puppet body language to show emotion (slumping for sadness, shaking for fear, double-take for surprise) or eye contact (face the audience or another puppet). Then replay your script, adding puppet body language.

Remember: Help children to see that story happens through action and dialogue, rather than relying on narration.

Materials: Children's media books with predictable, active plots (e.g., Dora the Explorer, Bob the Builder); puppets with movable mouths and arms or legs (e.g., Muppet-style puppets or other plush puppets); YouTube videos for puppetry demonstrations that illustrate body language and eye contact such as:

- *Eye Contact for Puppeteers* at http://www.youtube.com/watch?v=swEa_rPFBfw
- *Body Language Tips for Puppeteers* at http://www.youtube.com/watch?v=BMM6LZaKA7g
- *Tips for Making Puppet Voices* at http://www.youtube.com/watch?v=CZLeYbca6Do

Technology Try-It: Digital Video Cameras

Digital video cameras can catch and play back action and dialogue so that children can see their puppets from an audience's perspective. These digital tools can supplement and enrich print-based storying as teachers scribe during shared writing sessions as children rewatch puppet stories.

Mapping Story in Film Shorts with Storyboards

In films, stories are made up of camera shots, which are made up of sequences of shots. By stopping and starting action, children can look closely at a key sequence to see how shots—and the relationships among shots—carry the story forward.

Pixar shorts are 2- to 5-minute computer animated films that make good mentor texts to show young filmmakers how to tell a story in film. Students may be familiar with the shorts, as many were bundled with Pixar's full-length feature films (*Toy Story* [Lasseter, 1995], *Cars* [Lasseter & Ranft, 2006]) or broadcast on Disney Channel or Toon Disney. Plus, some are available on YouTube or DVD. Several Pixar shorts are wordless stories that help children focus on the images in film to see how action carries the storyline. When showing films in the classroom, it's important to distinguish between entertainment purposes and fair use in education. To comply with U.S. fair use provisions in copyright law, be sure that you are showing only showing the film clips necessary for the *educational purpose*. Here film clips are viewed for the following educational purpose in media literacy:

Purpose: To analyze film as text and capture action from the film in a storyboard

Description: Pixar shorts such as *The Adventures of André & Wally B.* and *Luxo Jr.* (Lasseter, 1986) work well for whole-class viewing, as the length of these films allows children to quickly grasp the meaning during a 10- to 15-minute mini-lesson.

First watch a scene to understand the action. Then rewatch the clip with close-up vision, noticing the most important parts: What are the characters doing or trying to do? What happens or changes in this clip?

Have students share with a partner(s) the parts they remember. Make a collective list on a class chart.

Rewatch the scene and tell the children to give a thumbs-up when they notice a new part so that you can stop the film to allow them to share what they noticed.

Additional Ideas for Mini-lessons with Film Shorts

- Stop the film at regular intervals (e.g., every 20 seconds) to pair/share or turn and talk, having each child replay or retell each chunk of story with a partner to locate key sequences that carry the story.
- Watch one short film sequence and stop the film after a few seconds to talk about what is happening in a particular shot. Ask the children what they noticed and how they might analyze the film. (For example, while watching Luxo Jr., students might notice that in one shot you see two cords but only one lamp, giving a hint of another lamp.)
- Listen to the film, considering how the sound effects and music also tell the story.
- Watch the film, noticing facial expressions and postures. Imagine what the characters might be feeling or words they might want to say in the story.
- Choose a film sequence and demonstrate how to draw the shots that make up that sequence (i.e., draw as you retell a chunk of the film on a storyboard). Have the children draw along on whiteboards or lapboards.
- Invite the children to draw storyboard sequences for a new story of their own. Remember: Storyboards are tools for quickly capturing ideas, not polished products. Encourage the children to sketch out ideas rather than to draw and color carefully. Encourage variation—some students may choose to add words to represent the script or sound effects, whereas others may want to use only pictures to show what happens.

Materials:

- Short films without narration or dialogue to help students concentrate on how the image carries the action using the storyboard tool.
- Short films, such as toy or fast food commercials, for analyzing persuasive rather than narrative models to see how images work to make products attractive through sensory and emotional appeal.
- Examples of professional storyboards [e.g., Pixar storyboards (http://www.theanimationblog.com/2009/05/11/up-storyboards/) and Pixar storytellers explaining the storyboarding process in the video Toy Story—Storyboarding at http://www.youtube.com/watch?v=QOeaC8kcxH0)
- Resources on classroom fair use and U.S. copyright law:
    http://www.centerforsocialmedia.org/fair-use/related-materials/codes/
        code-best-practices-fair-use-media-literacy-education
    http://www.ala.org/tools/libfactsheets/alalibraryfactsheet07

Technology Try-It: Storyboards with Video Stills

Digitize children's play scenarios by capturing media play with a video camera for immediate playback. If you upload the video into iMovie or Movie Maker, you can create stills that can be used as the framework for a storyboard that can be revised, re-created, or both.

If you have an iPad 2 or other video-enabled digital tablet, you can use its camera feature to capture play. When you play the video, you can create a still shot of anything in the video by simultaneously pressing the "Power" and "Home" buttons. The photo is instantly stored in the Photos app. You can then print the photos or copy and paste them into a document so that children can arrange the shots into their own sequences and storyboards. (See live action still shots in figures below.)

Negotiating Meaning with Popular Media Toys

Popular media toys work especially well for prompting meaning negotiations because they bring familiar narratives and characters that children are excited to play and often know by heart. Using these toys as props gives children an anchor for storytelling and expedites play when all the children already know and agree upon a character's likely actions and dialogue.

Purpose: To help children cooperate as they tease out their individual understandings of media narratives and eventually work together to improvise new shared meanings

Description: Organize groups of three students, giving each group a plastic bag containing three small popular media toys (e.g., Happy Meal toys) and inviting the children to use the toys to play out stories.

Set the stage, as Doriet did when she explained, "Storytellers sometimes use props to tell a story. A prop is an object. I know when I've seen a play, where there's a baker in a scene, one of his props might be a rolling pin or a baker's hat." She pantomimed using these props with her hands. "So props are *objects* that help us to *tell stories*, and today, you and two other partners are going to get toys in a bag."

Set clear expectations for collaborative storying, as Doriet did: "And you are going to work together to tell a story that happens with those props, your toys. You will have at least ten minutes, but part of how we know what's a just-right amount of time is seeing how you're using that time. If all of you are *so* busy storytelling, we will make sure that you have more time. If it looks like you are getting finished, then that tells us it's time to come back together. But use whatever time you have to add to your story, and tell a story with your partners that is interesting to you. Okay?"

Circulate, stopping to listen as students plan their stories together. Mediate with questions or suggestions if children can't agree on who plays which toy, ignore some group members' ideas, become engrossed in their own toys, or get stuck on story action that dissolves into play fights between toys.

Respond to children's play as action texts, looking for meaning in all the variety that play provides. For example, some children enacted the roles themselves as extensions of their toys, moving around by "flying" or maneuvering dramatically in ways that toys could not.

Materials: Small bags with three (or four) toys, enough bags so that every child has a toy and can work with at least two other children.

Technology Try-It: Multiplayer Interaction on Touchscreens

If you have a touchscreen tablet (e.g., iPad), you can have small groups of three children collaborate to make an instant movie with an animation app (e.g., Toontastic in figure below). Have each child animate one character as they play and record a story together. These programs have the advantage of immediate playback and endless opportunities for "do-overs" if children want to revise. When they are finished, they can also save and show their stories to other small groups. Similarly, collaborative drawing apps such as Whiteboard Lite allow two children to draw together on a virtual shared screen while making drawings on individual tablets.

Editing Film and Creating Sound Effects

Meaning-making doesn't stop when the camera is turned off. After children record a film, they can use film editing software to layer more meanings onto their stories. Children can trim or rearrange clips to make sequences that are silly or sensible or mysterious. Similarly, they can create transitions between clips that are smooth or surprising. Narration, music, and sound effects can make the story more understandable, while title screens, subtitles, and credits make films more realistic. Movie editing software such as iMovie or Windows Movie Maker comes preloaded with visual effects that make neon blurs or sepia antique tones and sound effects that bring the story to life (and also mask unwanted noises or voices on a soundtrack). Karen's preschoolers became excited when she applied a neon outline visual effect to their Star Wars scene and made the children's cardboard lightsabers appear to glow (see figure below). Visual and sound effects draw children's attention to sensory details in their storying. Creating homemade sound effects allows young children to connect sound effects to real materials in the physical world.

Purpose: To explore and capture a variety of sounds for use in filmmaking

Description: With the whole class, ask the students to close their eyes and tell you what sound they hear as you crumple wax paper. (This should sound similar to fire crackling.) After listening to children's guesses, ask the students to open their eyes and show them the material used to make the sound. Explain that sound effects can stand for something real like a fire. But sound effects can also suggest a feeling or action. Children may know some of these meanings from cartoons (e.g., the action of tiptoeing is suggested by rapid tapping of one note on a xylophone).

After showing the students the materials you have collected, explain that they should explore how they can use these objects to re-create sounds for a movie (e.g., realistic such as the sound of a door closing or iconic such as the *boing* sound, made by the release of a compressed spring, that is often used to symbolize surprise). Then share examples of materials or actions and the sound effects they make, such as:

- 2 plastic cups sound like galloping when tapped mouth-down on a table
- Empty water bottle sounds like cracking when squeezed
- Old soft-soled leather shoe sounds like creeping feet when bent
- Tin canister filled with pebbles sounds like objects crashing when rolled
- Thin metal cookie sheet sounds like thunder when waved
- Musical instruments—xylophones, kazoos, bells, tambourines, finger chimes—-can make iconic sounds used in cartoons

After the students have had an opportunity to explore the sound possibilities of the objects, regroup, have the children share their discoveries and make a list of the sounds created.

Demonstrate how to record and play back the sounds so the children can record sounds themselves. After all sounds have been recorded, tell the students to continue producing and collecting sounds they might be able to use later. (Children can also make the sound effects offcamera during filming.)

Materials: Wax paper, xylophone (or any material to illustrate a sound effect); objects for exploration; digital recorder or tablet with audio recording app

Technology Try-It: Movie-making Apps

Record sound effects with digital recorders and copy the audio files to laptops so you can import the effects into Movie Maker or iMovie. Tablets make this process even simpler. Using current iPads, for example, children can record sound effects or create music using electronic instruments on the GarageBand app, a music-making app that transfers the audio track directly into a project in the iMovie app.

Meaning Mediators

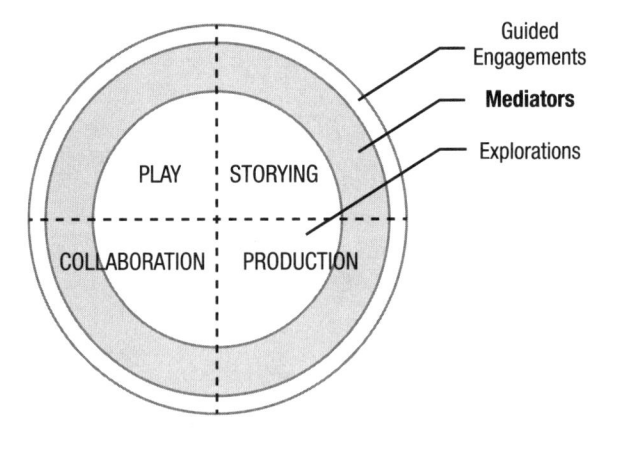

Mediators emerge from the shared meanings that children co-construct that come to stand for a character or an agreed-upon way of sharing the camera. The mediators that develop in your classroom may be very different from those in a classroom down the hall. Mediators include things and people but also ways of doing things such as scripts, rules, and routines. In this component, the description of each mediator addresses two questions: *what* illustrates the kinds of materials that make up this tool, and *why* explains the rationale for using it to mediate literacy play in your classroom.

Puppets and More

What: Puppets are proxies for co-constructed play narratives or student-authored stories. In the classrooms we observed, they ranged from purchased fleece or fur stuffed puppets to digital avatars to child-made paper puppets. Puppets can be original characters from student-created stories or popular media characters from television or film that students appropriate for their own versions.

Why: Puppets allow children to easily recognize who is playing which character, to anticipate dialogue with other actors, and to claim a specific role in the play narrative. Often children break out of character to negotiate the characters' next move in the story, sparking creative actions and improvisations.

Costumes and Props

What: Costumes and props can be anything that inspires a performance: old prom dresses, plastic fire helmets, or paper grocery sacks. Following a reading of *The Paper Bag Princess* (Munsch, 1980), Dawn and Michiru provided paper bags, scissors, tape, glue, foil, and markers to inspire the children to create paper suits of armor, swords, and shields to act out their own versions of the revisionist fairy tale.

Why: Children process and extend what they know about stories and the world through play, often making connections to their own lives or imagined life possibilities. Opportunities to create costumes, props, and sets invite remaking and add creative energy to dramatic reenactment.

Playsets and Dolls

What: Dolls (such as Barbie dolls, action figures, and inexpensive character figurines) and playsets (such as dollhouses, miniature villages, and Lego sets) are excellent mediators for exploring popular media storylines and themes.

Why: Simply allowing children to mix commercial playsets with classroom toys encourages inventive changes to popular media storylines. As described in Chapter 3, Dawn and Michiru invited the children to use *Toy Story* and *Dora the Explorer* action figures to see what play narratives would emerge. To enrich the storylines they imagined, the children combined media figurines with other materials from around the classroom—dollhouse toys, barnyard animals, cars, blocks, yarn—to construct sets and props for their characters. These combinations stretched the media narratives to accommodate children's ideas and experiences. Having media toys in the classroom proved to be a solid support that enabled children to carry a durable storyline from place to place and day to day.

Technology Try-It: Play Videos and Photoboards

What: Videos and photoboards (created from photographs and video stills) are visual tools for documenting children's play. Films of play scenarios can be paused for still shots, which can be printed on individual cards that children can use to retell, create a new story sequence, or revise on storyboards.

Why: Photoboards displayed on classroom walls enable children to revisit themes and to see their play as valued in the classroom. It also allows you and children to share their learning and the filmmaking process with families and other school visitors, other classes, and school supervisors and administrators.

Meaning Anchors

What: Dolls and puppets are not the only ways to represent play meanings. Children organize their play and anchor their hard-fought agreed-upon meanings with a variety of other tools such as scripts that show dialogue, cast lists that assign roles to particular players, or paper scenery that shows the planned scenes.

Why: Meaning anchors allow children to pick up where they left off, to extend the plot action, and to create more complex characters and storylines in which they do not need to retrace their steps or start anew each day. In our study, some kindergartners built elaborate sets that stretched across the width of the classroom. The locations pictured on these enormous sets also held children's shared ideas for action and dialogue—"You go here and then you say . . ."—as a visual reminder of what should occur when actors or puppets entered a particular section of the set.

Photo Puppets

What: Photos of children's faces can be used to personalize feltboard popular media characters (commercially produced or teacher-made felt cutouts) by placing Velcro on the back of cut-out laminated photos of children's faces. Children can then place their faces over various characters.

Why: Photo puppets encourage children to create stories in character and to add action and dialogue to their stories. In Karen and Sara's classroom, a group of girls personalized and juggled multiple roles simultaneously (e.g., one girl played Cinderella's stepmother, the father, and the stepsisters), switching back and forth between acting and using the photo puppets. The personalized felt photo puppet characters prompted the girls to use their best evil queen voices to command, "Capture them!," weaving story language in and out of their play.

Picture Books as Mentor Texts

What: Picture books with illustrations that carry the story, such as *Knuffle Bunny* (Willems, 2004) or *The Red Book* (Lehman, 2004), provide mentor texts for visual storying. Books like *Zoom* (Banyai, 1995) illustrate how story meanings are created with media production techniques like zoom in and zoom out. Picture books and beginning reading books often make common story structures explicit so that young readers can follow the story.

Why: Picture books bridge school curriculum and popular media filmmaking; they are also a readily available resource in most classrooms. Children can pore over wordless books and analyze illustrations as models of showing—not telling—characters, action, and setting. Elizabeth and Doriet wanted to help emergent readers connect their understanding of story structure in familiar children's literature to action sequences in storyboarding and film production, so they introduced three types of story patterns:

1. Action → Response or Result → Surprise/End [e.g., cause-effect cycle books such as *If You Give a Mouse a Cookie* (Numeroff, 1985)]
2. Beginning → Middle → End (e.g., fairy tales that have a once-upon-a-time beginning, followed by adventure and a happily-ever-after ending)
3. Beginning → +1 Event → End [e.g., cumulative stories that build, like *The Napping House* (Wood & Wood, 1994)]

After reading a book aloud, Elizabeth asked the students what type of pattern they thought the author used when writing the book. A large chart displayed pictures of the book covers and small (2-inch-x-2-inch) colored squares of paper to represent the pattern identified in the story. Using *It's Super Mouse!* (Root, 2002), students represented the story pattern with one brown square ("beginning") followed by five yellow squares ("middle"), one green square ("result"), and finally one blue square ("end"). This visual strategy of using color to represent the different parts of the story allowed all students to "read" the chart. This is in sharp contrast to text-heavy anchor charts that often exclude students who are not confident readers. Based on its success, Doriet and Elizabeth continued to use this language and color-coding scheme to highlight patterns found in student- and teacher-produced storyboards.

Animated Stories and Character Cut-Outs

What: Children can draw and cut out paper characters and animate them by pushing the cut-outs with their fingers across paper scenery.

Why: Cut-out animation aligns naturally with children's ideas about storying: the story moves along as the children move characters across scenes. The *Wow! Wow! Wubbzy!* animation described in Chapter 3 demonstrates this very easy animation technique. All that's needed is a cameraperson to film the action.

Technology Try-It: Digital Puppets

Animated stories with character cut-outs are easily created on touchscreen tablets using digital puppetry apps like Puppet Pals. Using a video-enabled tablet such as an iPad 2, children can take photos of themselves or favorite popular media figures or classroom toys; the photos then automatically appear in the Puppet Pals character list. Children can virtually "cut out" their photo puppets and use them as they move characters and record their voices in an animated puppet show, which can be saved and replayed. The figure below shows photo cutouts of classroom princess dolls imported into a pirate ship scene in the Puppet Pals app.

Why: Animated apps encourage collaboration as well as interactive storying, as they allow multiple players to simultaneously animate and coordinate characters on one touchscreen.

Time for Playing Together

What: Children need regular (every day), sustained (45 minutes) time to play together (in self-selected groups) with themes of their own choice and design, mediated by a thoughtful teacher.

Why: Play runs on collaboration. Play is built upon a shared agreement to pretend that classroom reality is something else. Because children's pretense is fluid— "Pretend I'm Dora and you're Diego"—it is also fragile, so children need to frequently check in and explain what their actions mean or what they should do next. This collaboration helps children anticipate how others interpret their intended meanings, fundamental perspective-taking that is crucial in writing.

Teachers as Mediators and Co-Players

What: The collaborative nature of play makes it an ideal place to challenge and remake prevalent media stereotypes, which suggests that teachers have an important role to play as well. Teachers can join children's play as co-players, adding depth within the play scenario by making suggestions and responding to children in character as Sara did when she played a fellow pirate in *The Pirate Movie*, always careful not to lead children's play themes but to contribute as a helpful follower.

Why: In this study, teachers were involved in children's play, stepping in and out as mediators, not only to settle disputes or ensure that children were not excluded, but as co-players to extend and enrich children's understandings of unfolding play narratives. Just as the presence of an adult who is sincerely interested in hearing a child's story or seeing a new discovery can fuel further exploration, a teacher who contributes a bit of dialogue as a fellow player can spark new interest in elaborating on or developing a story.

Peer Negotiation Structures

What: A classroom atmosphere of mutual respect, in which everyone's idea has merit, not only provides a strong foundation for collaborative work but creates the need to equitably resolve differences. Class meetings and cooperative early childhood conflict resolution structures, such as peer-to-peer friendship meetings or peace chairs that engage children in two-way perspective-taking, allow children to tell their side of the story (DeVries & Zan, 2012).

Why: Structures for shared decision-making and peer negotiation structures help children listen to each other to clarify and reach shared understandings. Elizabeth and Doriet set aside time at the end of the day for children to reflect, discuss, and role-play solutions to social issues and conflicts that arose.

Peer Experts

What: Recognize children as experts by posting a chart and having them place their names or photos under areas of expertise, whether knowledge about a particular media theme or skill in operating camera equipment, storytelling, or making sound effects. Look for opportunities to encourage children to consult the chart and call for a peer expert when questions arise during Playshop.

Why: Part of the power of the Playshop approach comes from putting children in the role of expert by allowing them to teach one another during play and produce texts in areas they know better than adults.

Class Heart Map and Audit Trail

What: A collective map of popular media interests can be created by expanding Georgia Heard's (1998) heart map (see Chapter 2) to include the media interests of the whole class. Asking children to contribute to a collective heart map helps identify the characters and media themes that children love and their areas of expertise. You can integrate a heart map into an audit trail (Vasquez, 2004), which is a visual trail of class learning throughout the year. Some items you might include in an audit trail are charts, photoboards, artwork, writing, scenery, and puppets. Share students' progress with families by posting photos of the audit trail's evolution throughout the year on class websites and blogs.

Why: Heart maps and audit trails document and act as windows into students' collective interests and shared learning.

Technology Try-It: Wordle

Similar to a heart map, typing each child's favorite characters and themes into a wordle (www.wordle.net) creates a comprehensive word cloud that shows the relative popularity of particular media franchises in your classroom. The words for popular franchises will appear as larger words in the wordle.

Digital Cameras, Tablets, and Apps

What: While your budget may dictate your possibilities, there have never been more child-friendly yet sophisticated technologies available for young children. Unfortunately, the inexpensive Flip video cameras we used are no longer manufactured; however, other companies still offer hand-held digital video cameras. We transferred video clips to laptops for in-class viewing with Windows Media Player or Apple QuickTime and for video editing using Windows Movie Maker or Apple iMovie. However, touchscreen tablets with simplified apps and icon-based navigation provide much more support for early childhood learners. A tablet with an integrated camera such as an iPad (second-generation or higher) will not only capture video by pushing one button but allow students to view and show video on the tablet screen and also drag and drop, move, and trim the same clips for film editing (through purchase of an additional app such as iMovie).

Why: Teachers in these classrooms used equipment operation and care as an opportunity for shared responsibility as well as rule-making and negotiations, deciding together where, when, and how many children should use a device in order to protect the equipment.

Technology Try-It: Directors' Commentaries

What: In a director's commentary, children can use the voice-over features in video editing apps or software to talk about the film they have produced. For example, VoiceThread is an app that enables voice-over commentary that students can share with others and allows viewers (including families) to record their responses.

Why: Directors' commentaries provide a way to make producers' decisions and thought processes explicit, not only to the audience but also to the children who made the film. This opportunity for children to self-reflect allows you to hear what children intended to convey through their films, what they discovered during filming, and how they feel about their filmmaking experiences. With these insights, you can tailor instruction to better respond to children's developing knowledge, skills, and dispositions.

Explorations

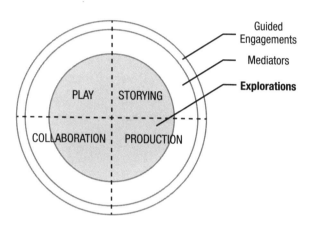

Explorations are child-led experiments and unpredictable discoveries that develop into learning and that inform teaching responses. Explorations feel a bit chaotic in the moment, but these tiny hands-on experiences develop skills for meaningful storying and production. This component presents a sampling of the variety of explorations that we observed so that you can anticipate the range of altogether unique explorations that may be invented by the children in your classroom.

Made Fresh Daily

Play is made fresh daily, yet with shared meanings that are anchored through toys, props, and familiar narratives. Although the theme may seem familiar, each replaying prompts more elaboration and new directions for stories. Children need regular and sustained opportunities to play so that they can revisit an idea over several play periods and improvise—switching roles, changing story action, adding characters, or inventing props, all ways of remaking commercial narratives.

Talking Hands

Expect unusual props. One play group used washable markers to decorate their hands and arms and used their hands to create characters. Positioning thumbs to move like "mouths," these inventive children used talking hands as actors in their filmmaking, capturing close-ups of their hands "talking" into the camera.

Using Cameras as Toys

Expect unexpected uses of tools. Children used cameras as characters and props by turning a hand-sized Flip camera into a doll and "walking" it across the table or using it like a building block: horizontally as Humpty Dumpty's wall or vertically as a skyscraper for King Kong to climb.

Playing Filmmaker

Appreciate play as a way of exploring a role. Children used cameras to play at being a director/cameraperson. They often just wanted to hold the camera, keeping it nearby as they or others played with toys. The camera was a role anchor that represented the authority to act as a director and tell others what to do. The intent here was to play at filmmaking (i.e., to make a pretend film of other children, even if the camera was not recording).

Animating with Paper, Scissors, and Tape

Allow children to construct characters and props. Children cut out drawings of characters or objects, transforming paper into puppets or props. The actions of cutting out, folding, or taping together bring an image to life by adding dimension.

For example, a 2-D drawing turns into a 3-D toy when paper is folded into an airplane that flies across the room or cut into a paper doll that bounces across a tabletop. Paper toys ranged in size from a hand-size Wubbzy to life-size puppets.

Technology Try-It: SkypePlay

Look for online play opportunities. SkypePlay uses social media to connect kindergartens and let children play together across the globe. Mardelle Sauerborn, a leading member of the Twitter community #kinderchat, invented SkypePlay with other kindergarten teachers around the world to allow children to play together across the Internet using real-time video on laptops to connect their classrooms. In the following SkypePlay video posted by Sauerborn, two boys explain their play scenario to Skype playmates as they enact being scientists while building "a volcano and a rocket ship" from toilet paper tubes and masking tape: http://prezi.com/xeklzhmrleg1/connecting-communities/.

Respecting Storying as an Exploratory Process

Each day in Literacy Playshop is a new opportunity for story creation through playing, drawing, and set construction. For young children, revision often occurs through repetition. In play themes, this means reworking an idea or character in a new context; in storying, this means starting over with a fresh piece of paper rather than changing something on an existing page. Communicate to students that it's okay to move on without "finishing" a storyboard. The focus should be on storyboards as tools in the filmmaking process rather than as neatly completed products. There seems to be little benefit from forcing children to go back to old storyboards, as this drained the improvisational energy out of their replaying and rewritings. In short, children need to be able to decide when to stop.

Sequencing Storyboards

Give children freedom to explore ways to sequence their stories, such as cutting apart storyboard panels so they can rearrange the shots in ways that are most meaningful to them. A group of boys in the K/1 class who were trying to collaborate on a storyboard found it easier if each boy worked on a separate storyboard rather than drawing simultaneously on one sheet of paper. When they finished, each storyboard was cut into "pages," with the pages stacked in order and then stapled on the left side. On the back of each small "book," the boys labeled whether it was part 1, 2, or 3.

Making Scenery with Propped-Up Books

Make books widely available. Children propped up books behind puppets and toys as ready-made sets for puppet shows and films. Students paged through picture books, even nonfiction texts, looking for background scenery for a film. Similarly, stories could be retold by leaning books against a wall and using each page as a different scene with toys or paper cut-outs enacting the story action.

Storying with Illustrations and Stills

Provide interesting illustrations from picture books and photo stills and screenshots from films. In the K/1 classroom, illustrations from wordless books such as David Weisner's *Tuesday* (Weisner, 1991) inspired ideas for new storylines and film settings. (See photo still from a child's film in figure below.)

Technology Try-It: Commercial Media Screenshots

Digital photo stills and screenshots from commercial films, in particular, can provide a hands-on method for retelling, reordering, or combining familiar story elements as children mix and match and remix stills as shots in storyboard panels.

Exploring Ways to Collaborate

Whether in play, storying, or production, children explore ways of collaborating: sometimes taking turns, sometimes orchestrating their individual parts, and sometimes merging all their ideas into a complex storyline. For example, in one K/1 group, each student recorded his or her own version of the collaborative story on separate storyboards. Then, following a bit of negotiation, one storyteller in the group gave directions about what to put in each frame of their final composite storyboard.

Cooperating with Cameras

Recognize that cameras are catalysts for collaboration, creating the need for someone to operate the camera and others to play the story. Children found that a camera they placed on a tabletop or tripod often missed the action. Touchscreen tablets have larger screens that make it easier for several children to collaborate on a film at once, but their larger size makes these cameras more unwieldy for little hands and less stable on tripods.

Rewatching Together on Mobile Screens

Encourage children to instantly review their films with co-players or friends so they can see the effects of their explorations. The small mobile screens on Flip cameras were more effective in sparking talk about the moviemaking than larger screens on TVs and laptops, which required adult help to transfer the video. Preschool children enjoyed rewatching or relistening to their recordings immediately after filming ended. They often crowded around the camera, giggling and fascinated, to point to ordinary objects captured on the small screen (a friend's face, the classroom guinea pig, etc.). (See figure below.)

Help children rewatch their films with more children by viewing them on the bigger screen of a laptop. Spontaneous audiences would form and hover in front of the screen to get a good look, or organize themselves auditorium-style on the floor to watch films and comment on what they saw together.

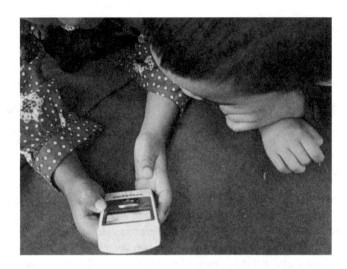

Technology Try-It: Projecting from Tablets to TVs

Wireless projection capabilities for tablets have evolved since the time of the study. For example, it would now be possible to show children's videos filmed on an iPad on a newer classroom television equipped with a wireless digital receiver such as Apple TV.

Bubbles of Filmmaking

The films that young children produce on their own are brief, playful, and repetitive explorations that approximate elements of filmmaking as children learn various aspects of multimodal media production. The figure below shows a bubble map that captures some of these elements—think fragile and temporary yet fascinating "bubbles" of experience—the children in our study explored in their tiny films.

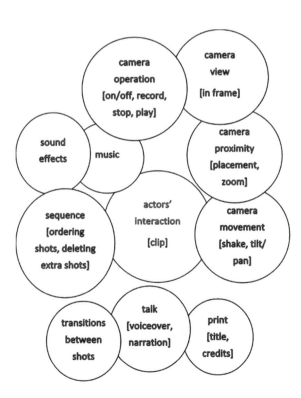

Seeing Like a Camera

Help children notice what the camera actually captures inside the frame. Preschoolers spent considerable time investigating what the camera "saw." Their investigations included:

- Moving stick puppets back and forth in front of a camera set on a tripod while seeing what the puppets looked like in the frame
- Moving the camera forward and backward while the filmed object or scene remained stationary
- Turning the camera sideways to film and view (as adults do with cameras and phones)
- Putting fingers and hands in front of camera while simultaneously holding the camera and viewing the recording

Making Sound Effects and Funny Voices

A recurring and popular exploration involved testing the microphone and sound recording function. Repetition and silly talk were key elements that gave this exploration its appeal and staying power. Children would ask friends to "say something" ("ooooo!," "Hello Mister! Hello Mister!," or "Chicken nugget, chicken nugget, chicken nugget") to the camera, which students would then play back and listen to immediately. Children combined pretense with equipment exploration, pretending the camera was a cell phone or microphone as they placed the camera next to their ears and mouths.

Pushing Buttons

In preschool, children often explored mechanical aspects of camera operation through repetitive movements: flipping the USB plug in and out of the Flip camera repeatedly, or pressing the Record or Power button on and off to see the effects on the viewing screen or the red recording light.

Technology Try-It: Wireless Microphones

When a toy microphone was placed in the dramatic play area, one preschooler constructed a sturdy "stage" made from big blocks and performed an impromptu variety show for his audience. Using gestures, dance moves, musical sounds, and voice quality he might have picked up from music competitions such as *American Idol*, he nodded to, chatted with, and worked the audience. He eventually recruited playmates to form a band with him, and they played a set on the stage and then paraded around the room with instruments they found in a toy bin. Using only the toy microphone as an initial mediator, the preschoolers created an entire play scenario that displayed knowledge of media production and sequences that quite realistically mimicked the staging of *American Idol*. This production shows how tiny moments of exploration bring together multiple processes and elements in a single film.

References

Allington, R., & Pearson, P. D. (2011). The casualties of policy on early literacy development. *Language Arts, 89*(1), 70–74.

Banyai, I. (1995). *Zoom.* New York: Viking.

Bazalgette, C. (2010). *Teaching media in primary schools.* London: Sage.

Boldt, G. M. (2002). Toward a reconceptualization of gender and power in an elementary classroom. *Current Issues in Comparative Education, 5*(1), 7–23.

Brown, E. (2009, November 21). The playtime's the thing. *The Washington Post.* Retrieved from http://www.washingtonpost.com/wp-dyn/content/article/2009/11/20/AR2009112002391.html

Buckingham, D. (2003). *Media education: Literacy, learning and contemporary culture.* Cambridge, UK: Wiley-Blackwell.

Calkins, L. M. (1994). *The art of teaching writing.* Portsmouth, NH: Heinemann.

Chapman, B., & Andrews, M. (Directors). (2012). *Brave.* Emeryville, CA: Pixar Animation.

Davies, B. (2003). *Frogs and snails and feminist tales: Preschool children and gender* (rev. ed.). Cresskill, NJ: Hampton Press.

DeVries, R., & Zan, B. (2012). *Moral classrooms, moral children: Creating a constructivist atmosphere in early education* (2nd ed.). New York: Teachers College Press.

Dyson, A. H. (2003a). *The brothers and sisters learn to write: Popular literacies in childhood and school cultures.* New York: Teachers College Press.

Dyson, A. H. (2003b). Popular literacies and the "all" children: Rethinking literacy development for contemporary childhoods. *Language Arts, 81*(2), 100–109.

Dyson, A. H. (2006). On saying it right (write): "Fix-its" in the foundations of learning to write. *Research in the Teaching of English, 41*(1), 8–42.

Dyson, A. H. (2008). Staying in the (curricular) lines: Practice constraints and possibilities in childhood writing. *Written Communication, 25*(1), 119–159.

Fernie, D., Madrid, S., & Kantor, R. (Eds.). (2011). *Educating toddlers to teachers: Learning to see and influence the school and peer cultures of classrooms.* Cresskill, NJ: Hampton Press.

Gee, J. P. (2010). *An introduction to discourse analysis: Theory and method* (3rd ed.). London: Routledge.

Göncü, A. (Ed.). (1999). *Children's engagement in the world: Sociocultural perspectives.* Cambridge, UK: Cambridge University Press.

Goodman, Y. M. (1978). Kidwatching: An alternative to testing. *National Elementary Principal, 57*(4), 41–45.

Grace, D. J., & Tobin, J. (1998). Butt jokes and mean-teacher parodies: Video production in the elementary classroom. In D. Buckingham (Ed.), *Teaching popular culture: Beyond radical pedagogy* (pp. 42–62). New York: Routledge.

Gutiérrez, K. D., & Rogoff, B. (2003). Cultural ways of learning: Individual traits or repertoires of practice. *Educational Researcher, 32*(5), 19–25.

Heard, G. (1998). *Awakening the heart.* Portsmouth, NH: Heinemann.

Heath, S. B. (1983). *Ways with words: Language, life, and work in communities and classrooms.* Cambridge, UK: Cambridge University Press.

Heffernan, L., & Lewison, M. (2005). What's lunch got to do with it? Critical literacy and the discourse of the lunchroom. *Language Arts, 83*(2), 107–116.

Knobel, M., & Wilber, D. (2009). Let's talk 2.0. *Educational Leadership, 66*(6), 20–24.

Kress, G. (1997). Before writing: Rethinking the paths to literacy. London: Routledge.

Kress, G. (2003). *Literacy in the new media age.* London: Routledge.

Lasseter, J. (Director). (1984). *The adventures of André & Wally B.* Emeryville, CA: Pixar Animation.

Lasseter, J. (Director). (1986). *Luxo Jr.* Emeryville, CA: Pixar Animation.

Lasseter, J. (Director). (1995). *Toy Story.* Emeryville, CA: Pixar Animation.

Lasseter, J., & Ranft, J. (Directors). (2006). *Cars.* Emeryville, CA: Pixar Animation.

Lehman, B. (2004). *The red book.* Boston, MA: Houghton Mifflin.

Lewison, M., Flint, A. S., & Van Sluys, K. (2002). Taking on critical literacy: The journey of newcomers and novices. *Language Arts, 79*(5), 382–392.

Long, M. (2003). *How I became a pirate* (D. Shannon, Illustrator). Orlando, FL: Harcourt.

Marr, K. (2008, July 30). Children targets of $1.6 billion in food ads. *The Washington Post.* Retrieved from http://www.washingtonpost.com/wp-dyn/content/article/2008/07/29/AR2008072902293.html

Marsh, J. (Ed.). (2005a). *Popular culture, new media and digital literacy in early childhood.* New York: RoutledgeFalmer.

Marsh, J. (2005b). Ritual, performance and identity construction: Young children's engagement with popular culture and media texts. In J. Marsh (Ed.), *Popular culture, new media and digital literacy in early childhood* (pp. 28–50). New York: RoutledgeFalmer.

Marsh, J. (2006). Popular culture in the literacy curriculum: A Bourdieuan analysis. *Reading Research Quarterly, 41*(2), 160–174.

Marsh, J. (2009). Productive pedagogies: Play, creativity, and digital cultures in the classroom. In R. Willett, M. Robinson, & J. Marsh (Eds.), *Play, creativity, and digital cultures* (pp. 200–218). New York: Routledge.

Marsh, J., Brooks, G., Hughes, J., Ritchie, L., Roberts, S., & Wright, K. (2005). *Digital beginnings: Young children's use of popular culture, media and new technologies* (Literacy Research Centre, The University of Sheffield Research Report). Retrieved from http://www.digitalbeginnings.shef.ac.uk/DigitalBeginningsReport.pdf

Martin, W., & Dombey, H. (2002). Finding a voice: Language and play in the home corner. *Language and Education, 16*(1), 48–61.

Medina, C. L., & Wohlwend, K. E. (In press). *Literacy, play, and globalization: Converging imaginaries in children's critical and cultural performances.* New York: Routledge.

Meyer, R. J., & Whitmore, K. F. (Eds.). (2011). *Reclaiming reading : Teachers, students, and researchers regaining spaces for thinking and action.* Mahwah, NJ: Erlbaum.

Munsch, R. (1980). *The paper bag princess*. Toronto: Annick.

Nixon, H., & Comber, B. (2005). Behind the scenes: Making movies in early years classrooms. In J. Marsh (Ed.), *Popular culture, new media and digital literacy in early childhood* (pp. 219–236). New York: RoutledgeFalmer.

Numeroff, L. J. (1985). *If you give a mouse a cookie*. Toronto: HarperCollins.

O'Keefe, T. (1997). The habit of kidwatching. *School Talk, 3*(2), 4–6.

Orr, L. (2009). "Difference that is actually sameness mass-reproduced": Barbie joins the princess convergence. *Jeunesse: Young People, Texts, Cultures, 1*(1), 9-30.

Pompe, C. (1996). "But they're pink!"—"Who cares!": Popular culture in the primary years. In M. Hilton (Ed.), *Potent fictions: Children's literacy and the challenge of popular culture* (pp. 92–125). London: Routledge.

Pugh, A. J. (2009). *Longing and belonging: Parents, children, and consumer culture*. Berkeley: University of California Press.

Ravitch, D. (2010). *The death and life of the great American school system*. New York: Basic Books.

Riddle, J. (2009). *Engaging the eye generation: Visual literacy strategies for the K–5 classroom*. Portland, ME: Stenhouse.

Rogow, F. (2002). ABC's of media literacy: What can pre-schoolers learn? *Telemedium: The Journal of Media Literacy, 48*(2).

Root, P. (2002). *It's super mouse!* Somerville, MA: Candlewick.

Sawyer, R. K. (1997). *Pretend play as improvisation: Conversation in the preschool classroom*. Norwood, NJ: Erlbaum.

Schoenberg, N. (2010, September 4). Kindergarten: It's the new first grade. *Chicago Tribune*. Retrieved from http://articles.chicagotribune.com/2010-09-04/features/sc-fam-0905-kindergarten-20100904_1_kindergarten-full-day-programs-early-grades

Seiter, E. (1992). Toys are us: Marketing to children and parents. *Cultural Studies, 6*(2), 232–247.

Sherzer, J. (2002). *Speech play and verbal art*. Austin: University of Texas Press.

Stipek, D. (2004). Teaching practices in kindergarten and first grade: Different strokes for different folks. *Early Childhood Research Quarterly, 19*(4), 548–568.

Swalwell, K., & Apple, M. W. (2011). Reviewing policy: Starting the wrong conversations: The public school crisis and "Waiting for Superman." *Educational Policy, 25*(2), 368-382.

Unkrich, L. (Director). (2010). *Toy Story 3*. Emeryville, CA: Pixar Animation.

U.S. Department of Education. (2011, April 21). *Why use transmedia in early learning?* Retrieved from http://www.ed.gov/oii-news/why-use-transmedia-early-learning-0

Vasquez, V. M. (2004). *Negotiating critical literacies with young children*. Mahwah, NJ: Erlbaum.

Vasquez, V. M., & Felderman, C. B. (2012). *Technology and critical literacy in early childhood*. New York: Routledge.

Volk, D., & Long, S. (2005). Challenging myths of the deficit perspective: Honoring children's literacy resources. *Young Children, 60*(6), 12–19.

Vygotsky, L. S. (1978). *Mind in society: The development of higher psychological processes* (M. Cole, V. John-Steiner, S. Scribner, & E. Souberman, Eds. & Trans.). Cambridge, MA: Harvard University Press. (Original work published 1935)

Wertsch, J. V. (2001). The multivoicedness of meaning. In M. Weterell, S. Taylor, & S. J. Yates (Eds.), *Discourse theory and practice* (pp. 222–235). London: Sage Publications.

Wiesner, D. (1991). *Tuesday.* Boston, MA: Houghton Mifflin

Willems, M. (2004). *Knuffle Bunny: A cautionary tale.* New York: Hyperion Books for Children.

Willett, R. (2008). "What you wear tells a lot about you": Girls dress up online. *Gender and Education, 20*(5), 421–434.

Wohlwend, K. E. (2005). Chasing friendship: Acceptance, rejection, and recess play. *Childhood Education, 81*(2), 77–82.

Wohlwend, K. E. (2009). Dilemmas and discourses of learning to write: Assessment as a contested site. *Language Arts, 86*(5), 341–351.

Wohlwend, K. E. (2010). A is for avatar: Young children in literacy 2.0 worlds and literacy 1.0 schools. *Language Arts, 88*(2), 144–152.

Wohlwend, K. E. (2011). *Playing their way into literacies: Reading, writing, and belonging in the early childhood classroom.* New York: Teachers College Press.

Wohlwend, K. E. (2012). The boys who would be princesses: Playing with identity intertexts in Disney Princess transmedia. *Gender and Education.* doi: 10.1080/09540253.2012.674495

Wohlwend, K. E., & Hubbard, P. (2011). Reclaiming play: Reading toys as popular media texts. In R. J. Meyer & K. F. Whitmore (Eds.), *Reclaiming reading: Teachers, students, and researchers regaining spaces for thinking and action* (pp. 241–255). Mahwah, NJ: Erlbaum.

Wohlwend, K. E., & Norton-Meier, L. A. (2007, November). *Making sense with and of Happy Meal toys, popular media, and technology: Seizing opportunities for language and literacy development.* Paper presented at the annual meeting of the National Association for the Education of Young Children, Chicago, IL.

Wood, A. & Wood, D. (1994). *The napping house.* San Diego: Harcourt Brace.

Index

About the Authors

Karen E. Wohlwend is an assistant professor in the Literacy, Culture, and Language Education Department in the School of Education at Indiana University. Her research reconceptualizes play as a literacy for reading and writing identity texts and as a tactic for participating and learning in early childhood classrooms. Wohlwend is the author of *Playing Their Way into Literacies: Reading, Writing, and Belonging in the Early Childhood Classroom* as well as numerous articles and chapters that provide a critical perspective on children's play and new literacies, popular media, gender, and identity.

Beth A. Buchholz is a doctoral student in the Literacy, Culture, and Language Education Department in the School of Education at Indiana University.

Linda Skidmore Coggin is a doctoral student in the Literacy, Culture, and Language Education Department in the School of Education at Indiana University.

Nicholas E. Husbye is an assistant professor in the College of Education at the University of Missouri—St. Louis.

Christy Wessel Powell is a doctoral student in the Literacy, Culture, and Language Education Department in the School of Education at Indiana University.